New Directions for
Higher Education

Martin Kramer and
Judith Block McLaughlin
CO-EDITORS-IN-CHIEF

Institutionalizing Community Engagement in Higher Education: The First Wave of Carnegie Classified Institutions

Lorilee R. Sandmann
Courtney H. Thornton
Audrey J. Jaeger
EDITORS

Number 147 • Fall 2009
Jossey-Bass
San Francisco

INSTITUTIONALIZING COMMUNITY ENGAGEMENT IN HIGHER
EDUCATION: THE FIRST WAVE OF CARNEGIE CLASSIFIED INSTITUTIONS
Lorilee R. Sandmann, Courtney H. Thornton, Audrey J. Jaeger (eds.)
New Directions for Higher Education, no. 147
Martin Kramer, Judith Block McLaughlin, Co-Editors-in-Chief

Microfilm copies of issues and articles are available in 16mm and 35mm,
as well as microfiche in 105mm, through University Microfilms Inc., 300
North Zeeb Road, Ann Arbor, MI 48106-1346.

NEW DIRECTIONS FOR HIGHER EDUCATION (ISSN 0271-0560, electronic
ISSN 1536-0741) is part of The Jossey-Bass Higher and Adult Education
Series and is published quarterly by Wiley Subscription Services, Inc.,
A Wiley Company, at Jossey-Bass, 989 Market Street, San Francisco, CA
94103-1741. Periodicals Postage Paid at San Francisco, California, and
at additional mailing offices. POSTMASTER: Send address changes to
New Directions for Higher Education, Jossey-Bass, 989 Market Street, San
Francisco, CA 94103-1741.

New Directions for Higher Education is indexed in Current Index to Journals in Education (ERIC); Higher Education Abstracts.

SUBSCRIPTIONS cost $89 for individuals and $244 for institutions, agencies,
and libraries. See ordering information page at end of journal.

EDITORIAL CORRESPONDENCE should be sent to the Co-Editors-in-Chief,
Martin Kramer, 2807 Shasta Road, Berkeley, CA 94708-2011 and Judith
Block McLaughlin, Harvard GSE, Gutman 435, Cambridge, MA 02138.

Cover photograph © Digital Vision

www.josseybass.com

CONTENTS

EDITORS' NOTES

In 1996 Ernest Boyer exalted American colleges and universities as "one of the greatest hopes for intellectual and civic progress in this country." But, he went on to say, ". . .for this hope to be fulfilled, the academy must become a more vigorous partner in the search for answers to our most pressing social, civic, economic and moral problems, and must reaffirm its historic commitment to what I call the scholarship of engagement" (pp. 19–20). As institutions of higher education entered the twenty-first century, they moved to respond to this challenge. Colleges and universities in the United States increasingly turned to community engagement as a natural evolution of their traditional missions of service to recognize ties to their communities along with their commitments to the social contract between society and higher education.

To demonstrate that it is critical for higher education to become engaged with its community in authentic, mutually beneficial partnerships, this volume eschews the usual arguments and presents the first large-scale "stocktaking" about the nature and extent of institutionalization of engagement in higher education. To what extent have higher education institutions become "engaged"? To what extent has the academy fulfilled hopes that it can be a vigorous partner in the search for answers to our most pressing social, civic, economic, and moral problems? The authors in this volume assess the progress by analyzing the first wave of what have been classified as community-engaged institutions by the Carnegie Foundation for the Advancement of Teaching (CFAT).

Carnegie Classification for Community Engagement

The Carnegie Foundation's recent development of the elective Community Engagement Classification has given this topic precedence among concerns of the higher education community. In 2006, the CFAT first offered its new elective classification as part of its classification system of postsecondary institutions. The first such elective classification was in community engagement, a term that, according to CFAT (2008), "describes the collaboration between institutions of higher education and their larger communities (local, regional/state, national, global) for the mutually beneficial exchange of knowledge and resources in a context of partnership and reciprocity." Its use is based on the voluntary participation by postsecondary institutions that wish to recognize, publicize, and share best practices about community

1

engagement as important elements of their strategically planned and managed missions. According to the Campus Compact (2008) of Brown University, ". . .This Carnegie classification reaffirms institutional commitment to deepen the practice of service and to further strengthen bonds between campus and community. . . ."

The actual classification has three categories of recognition. *Curricular engagement* applies to institutions where teaching, learning, and scholarship engage faculty, students, and community in collaborations with the intention of addressing community-identified needs, deepening students' civic and academic learning, enhancing community well-being, and enriching the scholarship of the institution. *Outreach and partnerships* applies to institutions that provided compelling evidence of one or both of two approaches to community engagement: outreach that features the application and provision of institutional resources for community use and partnerships that focus on collaborative interactions with community and related scholarship for the mutually beneficial exchange, exploration, and application of knowledge, information, and resources (for example, research, capacity building, and economic development). In the third categorization, institutions that show substantial commitment to both areas could be awarded classifications in both categories.

To date, 195 public and private institutions of higher education have submitted successful voluntary applications to CFAT documenting their experience in and commitment to community engagement. This volume analyzes data from the seventy-six institutions designated during the initial offering of this classification in 2006: sixty-two institutions were awarded the classification in both curricular engagement and outreach and partnerships, five were awarded only the curricular engagement classification, and nine were awarded only the outreach and partnerships classification. These institutions are geographically distributed around the United States, with particular clustering in the Northeast, Midwest, and California.

Because of its voluntary nature, the elective classification does not represent a comprehensive national assessment. Carnegie (2007) cautions that "an institution's absence from the Community Engagement classification should not be interpreted as reflecting a judgment about the institution's commitment to its community." However, this first wave of Carnegie community-engaged classified institutions can reveal much about the general state of engagement across types of higher education institutions and functions and about particular best practices. Of the seventy-six successful institutions, representing all types of classified institutions, fifty-six agreed to make their applications available for the research purposes of this volume. We found the application materials of these institutions filled with impressive examples of institutionalization and innovative activities. Taken as a whole, the submissions reveal areas of national strength, such as service-learning, as well as widespread areas of weaknesses, such as support for engagement in tenure and reward policies. This first wave offers us a unique opportunity to provide an analysis that will instruct leaders across all types of institutions on the current status of higher education outreach and engagement.

Contents of the Volume

The organization of this volume roughly corresponds to the broad categories of the Carnegie classification framework. The framework is extensive and requires institutions to report on foundational indicators (mission, policy, and so forth), curricular engagement, and outreach and partnerships. Within these three categories are more detailed discussions, including institutional identity and culture, leadership, resource allocations, policy, assessment, rewards and recognition, scholarship, and reciprocity. We have assembled key scholars and leaders in community engagement as chapter authors.

In Chapter One, Amy Driscoll more fully describes the classification: what it is, how it came to be, overall findings from the first wave, and updates from the 2008 process. One finding is that the role of leadership was critical for these engaged institutions. In Chapter Two, Lorilee Sandmann and William Plater examine ways that institutions and individuals serve in leadership roles for higher education community engagement.

Supportive environments for faculty who define their work as engaged scholarship is a persistent issue of discussion and discord. To better understand institutional reward policies and practices related to community engaged scholarship, John Saltmarsh, Dwight Giles Jr., Elaine Ward, and Suzanne Buglione present in Chapter Three an analysis based on the data from the campus applications as well as from the actual promotion and tenure guidelines for each campus. Their findings provide insight into nationwide faculty reward policies and practices for community engaged scholarship.

In Chapter Four, Robert Bringle and Julie Hatcher feature innovative practices in service-learning and curricular engagement. Rigorous and meaningful assessment of community engagement efforts, including in service-learning, continues to pose a challenge for institutions across the country. In Chapter Five, Andrew Furco and William Miller, leaders on national task forces to develop systems for benchmarking and assessing engagement, explore the institution-level challenges in tracking and assessing outreach and engagement. Because of the diversity in types of engagement and the scope and scale of engagement within and across campuses, single institutions and nationwide organizations have been challenged to develop a set of metrics for assessing engagement.

In Chapter Six Carole Beere considers outreach and partnerships and addresses the important issue of the community partner in institutional planning and implementation of engagement efforts.

This is followed by consideration of the progress and challenges in funding engagement efforts. David Weerts and Elizabeth Hudson share in Chapter Seven the ways in which engaged institutions allocate internal resources to support engagement and how these campuses have reshaped their institutional advancement programs through such activities as marketing, branding, and fundraising to leverage financial support for engagement.

The Carnegie community engagement application process and its data can also serve as a vehicle for institutionalizing engagement. Courtney Thornton and James Zuiches examine in Chapter Eight the North Carolina State University process and application findings through an organization theory lens. This perspective helps campuses take a "50,000 foot" view of the vast data collected for the Carnegie process in order to craft useful recommendations for the institution and to sustain an institution's wave of energy for this topic after the classification.

The penultimate chapter is an overall assessment of the institutionalization of community engagement by Barbara Holland, who discusses exemplary and varying ways in which engagement is becoming embedded in institutional foundations and the strategic directions of higher education organizations with different missions.

In the final chapter, we, the volume editors, discuss overall themes, best practices, outstanding issues, and future directions brought to the light by this first wave of classified institutions in community engagement.

Lorilee R. Sandmann
Courtney H. Thornton
Audrey J. Jaeger
Editors

References

Boyer, E. L. "The Scholarship of Engagement." *Journal of Public Service and Outreach,* 1996, *1*(1), 9–20.

Campus Compact. "Civic Engagement Initiatives." 2008. Retrieved June 1, 2008, from http://www.compact.org/initiatives/civic_engagement/.

Carnegie Foundation for the Advancement of Teaching. "Elective Classification: Community Engagement—2008 Documentation Framework." 2007. Retrieved June 1, 2008, from http://www.carnegiefoundation.org/dynamic/downloads/file_1_614.pdf.

Carnegie Foundation for the Advancement of Teaching. "Community Engagement." 2008. Retrieved June 1, 2008, from http://www.carnegiefoundation.org/classifications/index.asp?key=1213.

LORILEE R. SANDMANN *is associate professor in the Department of Lifelong Education, Administration and Policy at the University of Georgia and director of the National Review Board for the Scholarship of Engagement.*

COURTNEY H. THORNTON *is director of research for the University of North Carolina system.*

AUDREY J. JAEGER *is associate professor of higher education and founder of the Center for Research on Engagement at North Carolina State University.*

1

The new Carnegie classification of community engagement provides a unique opportunity for campuses to embrace their responsibilities to society.

Carnegie's New Community Engagement Classification: Affirming Higher Education's Role in Community

Amy Driscoll

In 2005, the Carnegie Foundation for the Advancement of Teaching (CFAT) stirred the higher education world with the announcement of a new classification for institutions that engage with community. The classification, community engagement, is the first in a set of planned classification schemes resulting from the foundation's reexamination of the traditional Carnegie classification system. The new classifications are intended to provide flexibility, closer match of data with purpose, and a multidimensional approach for better representing institutional identity. The first of those new schemes, community engagement, has prompted a flurry of inquiry, self-assessment, documentation, and development of engagement practices as educators in colleges and universities strive to qualify for the classification.

Introduction to the Classification

The community engagement classification affirms that a university or college has institutionalized engagement with community in its identity, culture, and commitments. The classification further affirms that the practices of community engagement have been developed to the extent that they are aligned with the institutional identity and an integral component of the institutional culture. This classification is elective: it relies on voluntary participation by an institution. In contrast to the traditional Carnegie classification, which uses national data, the community engagement classification uses documentation provided by each institution.

NEW DIRECTIONS FOR HIGHER EDUCATION, no. 147, Fall 2009 © Wiley Periodicals, Inc.
Published online in Wiley InterScience (www.interscience.wiley.com) • DOI: 10.1002/he.353

The term *community engagement* was intentionally selected for the classification to encompass the broadest conception of interactions between higher education and community and to promote inclusivity. The definition of *community engagement* used for the classification also represents broad thinking about collaborations between higher education and the community and intentionally encourages important qualities such as mutuality and reciprocity. The definition serves as an initial guide to both documentation and review processes for the classification: *community engagement* describes the collaboration "between higher education institutions and their larger communities (local, regional/state, national, global) for the mutually beneficial exchange of knowledge and resources in a context of partnership and reciprocity."

Development and Initiation of the Community Engagement Classification

For many higher education professionals and community partners, the classification represented a unique opportunity to affirm the labors of many institutions and their partners to attend to Ernest Boyer's (1990, 1996) urging to embrace their responsibilities to society. Thus, its development was approached with the utmost reflection in terms of both intentions and content.

Intentions of the Classification. The vision for the classification was developed collaboratively by Carnegie colleagues and national engagement leaders and served as a significant guide for developing the documentation framework that institutions would use to apply for the classification. From its inception, the documentation framework was designed to respect the diversity of institutions and their approaches to community engagement; engage institutions in a process of inquiry, reflection, and self-assessment; and honor institutions' achievements while promoting the ongoing development of their programs (Driscoll, 2008). In addition, the development priorities attended to practicality and usefulness of data so that institutional documentations would be appropriate for such multiple purposes as program improvement and accreditation.

Development Processes for the Classification. From the beginning, the processes for developing a documentation framework for the community engagement classification built on concurrent developments for support. The ongoing benchmarking and assessment approaches of Campus Compact, the Council of Independent Colleges, the National Association of State Universities and Land-Grant Colleges, the Community-Campus Partnerships for Health, and individual institutions contributed substantive direction and examples. At the same time as those approaches were reviewed, intense consultation with national leaders highlighted challenges, potential, and priorities for the new classification and its documentation.

The earliest draft of the community engagement documentation framework integrated insights from the current literature base with those sources of consultation and current efforts. From there, Carnegie sponsored a pilot study of documentation with representatives of thirteen institutions of higher education. The representatives initially met to review and revise the documentation draft before engaging in a six-month trial of reporting and documenting community engagement at their respective institutions. After using the documentation framework, the group came together a second time to describe their individual campus experiences and synthesize recommendations for further revision of the framework. Each institution experienced new challenges and questions, as did the revision process for the documentation.

In the final revision process, there was unanimous support for some components of the documentation framework to serve as indicators of community engagement regardless of the diversity of institutions: institutional mission specifying community engagement as a priority, executive leadership that specifically promoted engagement, coordinating infrastructures and budgetary support for community engagement, and faculty development support for those engaged with community. There was also dissent among the pilot institutions about some indicators: search and recruitment policies and practices that support hiring of faculty with expertise and commitment to community engagement, and promotion and tenure policies that reward the scholarship of engagement. A number of representatives in the pilot study supported those indicators for the classification but simultaneously acknowledged that their own campuses could not qualify with such a requirement.

The resulting documentation framework was comprehensive, designed to capture the scope of institutional engagement, inclusive to affirm the diversity of approaches, and rigorous in promoting quality practices of community engagement. The framework would require many campuses to develop new data sources; however, it did encourage use of existing data for practicality reasons.

The Community Engagement Classification Framework

The documentation framework for the new classification was designed with two major components. In the first component, colleges and universities are expected to demonstrate institutionalization of community engagement, demonstrated through indicators of institutional identity and culture and institutional commitment. In the second component, they identify the focus of their community engagement: curricular engagement, outreach and partnerships, or both. This second component requires data, description, and examples of either or both of the focuses.

The documentation process is intensive and requires the collaboration of many institutional and community participants. It has often promoted new communication and cooperation across campuses and with community for data sharing and documentation.

Institutions that are able to document either or both of the categories of community engagement after demonstrating the foundational indicators are clearly deeply engaged with community.

Inaugural Applications—Process and Findings

The inaugural application of community engagement was approached with some trepidation and concern for the untried nature of the classification process, so the application pool was limited to ensure a thorough and reflective review process. A national advisory panel of engagement leaders representing varied institutions and national organizations was selected to support and enhance the review process. The panel also studied the initial applications and review process to inform revision of the classification process and documentation framework.

Profile of Inaugural Institutions Classified as Community Engaged. The initial response to the first application process came from 145 institutions early in 2006. Of those, 107 were selected to apply based on diversity of institutional size, institutional type, program emphasis, and location. By September 2006, eighty-nine institutions submitted full documentation for review. Those that did not submit applications described a lack of readiness for documentation or a need for further development of their engagement practices. When the newly classified institutions were announced in December 2006, seventy-six colleges and universities, representing a broad range of institutional type and size, were classified as institutions of community engagement.

As hoped and expected, the seventy-six institutions documented widely varied approaches to community engagement. Strong documentations exhibited clear alignment between the foundational indicators, such as mission, leadership, budgetary support, and strategic plan. They described supportive infrastructures in different forms, faculty development in a wide range of strategies, and diverse and creative ways of involving the community in the institution, all of which were compelling evidence of institutional commitment. Another distinction that was noted across the newly classified institutions was a difference in the conceptualization of both community and community engagement. Indiana University-Purdue University, Indianapolis is committed to the concept of civic engagement and documented its commitments and activity according to its philosophical stance. North Carolina State University introduced its documentation with a definition of community unlike Carnegie's geographical concept to better reflect the scope of campus activities. Its definition included "identifiable groups of individuals that share similar interests, concerns, and educational needs around a subject-matter area" (Zuiches and others, 2008, p. 43).

Among the seventy-six classified institutions, five documented only curricular engagement, and nine focused their documentation on outreach and partnerships. Sixty-two institutions documented both categories of engagement for the classification. Within the documentation of curricular engagement, institutions described different definitions of service-learning, varied integration within campuswide programs, and multiple forms of faculty scholarship related to curricular engagement. Within outreach and partnerships, the institutions described diverse partnerships in terms of disciplinary focus, size, length of time, and purposes and extensive examples of related faculty scholarship.

The decisions of whether to classify individual institutions was a careful process conducted by Carnegie staff and supported by the national advisory panel of leaders in community engagement nationally. It was important during the initiation of the classification process to have multiple perspectives considered in the decision-making process. The panel provided those perspectives on individual applications and at the same time reflected on the documentation framework and the overall application process. Their feedback was a substantive source of revision prior to the 2008 classification application process.

Institutional Perspectives on Impact of Classification. Many of the newly classified institutions achieved instant recognition and visibility when the Carnegie Foundation announced the inaugural group of successfully classified institutions for 2006. For states like Kentucky, in which there was statewide accountability for community engagement, the classification served as a kind of report card. For institutions with the intent of establishing an identity related to community engagement, there was the Carnegie acknowledgment of their focus. Within months after the announcement, institutional brochures and flyers clearly contained this recognition with the university message. A number of institutional representatives reported that the process of documentation revealed both gaps and strengths, often motivating renewed development or internal recognition. The self-assessment or self-study intent of the classification framework prompted many institutions to expand or initiate tracking and assessment systems and strategies.

Reflections on Community Engagement in the Context of the 2006 Classification

A review of the strengths and challenges acknowledged by institutions in their documentation provides clear direction for institutions committed to community engagement. This chapter focuses on the challenges—institutional recording and assessment systems and approaches, revision of promotion and tenure policies and practices, and communication and collaboration with community—because they are applicable to most institutions and have significant potential for improving community engagement in general.

Assessment of Community Engagement. Assessment in general continues to be an ongoing challenge for higher education, so it is not surprising that assessment of community engagement is in dire need of development. Even the simple tracking and recording of engagement activities appeared to be difficult to maintain with a systematic institution-wide process. Few institutions could be specific about institution-wide student learning outcomes related to engagement, so most assessment of curricular engagement took the form of individual course assessments and occasional program assessment. (Bringle and Hatcher discuss this idea further in Chapter Four.) Most institutions relied on data from individual faculty projects and some departmental reviews to document their community engagement approaches, but few examples of consistent assessment of community engagement were found.

As we expand community engagement across institutions of higher education, it is essential to develop the expertise and resources to assess and evaluate practices. Community engagement requires extensive resources, especially faculty time commitments, so it is imperative to assess well to articulate clarity of direction for these efforts and to ensure that this work is effectively achieving its intentions.

Promotion and Tenure Policies Supporting Community Engagement. This area of challenge is not a surprise to any professional who has engaged with community, but it was discouraging to find so few examples of revised recognition and reward systems for promotion and tenure. A standard response in the data was that institutions encouraged faculty to include community engagement scholarship in the service category, but that traditional scholarship was the real requirement for promotion and tenure.

All institutions described faculty development support for community engagement, but few documented that the work was a priority in their recruitment and hiring practices. When these gaps—lack of reward and recognition and lack of priority in hiring—are viewed in the context of a strong set of foundational indicators (for example, mission, budget, infrastructure), the inconsistency is disturbing.

Changes in the long-standing tradition of promotion and tenure policies and conceptualizations of scholarship are not easily achieved, as evidenced in the 2006 data. However, if, as the Carnegie classification indicates, community engagement has become an integral component of the role of institutions of higher education, then efforts to make such changes must be accelerated. It has been clearly established in the community engagement literature (Driscoll, 2000; O'Meara and Rice, 2005) that faculty are key to engaged institutions, and therefore supporting them with promotion and tenure policies is long overdue

Communication and Collaboration with Community. A significant area of challenge appeared first in the foundational indicators and was prominent in the outreach and partnerships section: communication and collaboration with community. Initially institutions struggled to describe how they assessed community perceptions of the institution and how the institution responded to the community. Later in the foundational indicators, institutions were asked to describe the role of community in agenda setting and decision making regarding community engagement. The differences in the responses to both of these foundational indicators were stark, with some institutions describing wide-ranging strategies and substantive community roles. Other institutions described infrequent or annual small-scale, formal processes with minimal representation of community or limited impact on institutional affairs.

Later in the documentation, when institutions listed and described partnerships with community, they were asked about maintaining reciprocity and systematic feedback in those partnerships. Most institutions could describe only in vague generalities how reciprocity was achieved, and few examples of systematic feedback were found in the data. These levels of involvement with community clearly demand new understandings, new skills, and even a new way of conceptualizing community, and typically with little advance preparation for faculty or administrators. This is another area in which tradition may be blocking progress, as institutions of higher education shed the long-standing ivory tower image and, sometimes, reality.

Conclusion

All of the areas of challenge spotlight the work to be done in higher education if community engagement is to truly be integral to the identity of higher education in the United States. The national recognition of a Carnegie classification has enhanced both the prominence and potential of community engagement in colleges and universities. If that prominence is to be authentic and the potential is to be achieved, higher education must address gaps in assessment and evaluation of community engagement, support for key faculty roles in community engagement with aligned search and hiring practices and promotion and tenure policies, and improved communication and collaboration with community as partners.

At the time of this writing, 154 applications for the 2008 classification were under review. The documentation framework used for the 2008 application process was almost identical to the 2006 framework. There was minimal editing after the initiation and only minimal additions. The 2008 process was, however, completely electronic, and the application process was simpler. A major difference for institutions in 2008 was that the entire documentation framework was available on the Carnegie Web site for a significant period before the application deadlines. The intent of that availability was to support institutions in making a decision about whether to apply. It is surprising that seventy institutions withdrew from the application process just prior to the final deadline, most frequently citing "lack of readiness for qualifying for the classification" as the reason.

It is anticipated that this new round of applications for the Carnegie classification will produce additional insights about the practices of community engagement and will provide significant documentation of progress toward the potential for higher education's role in community.

The application data will undoubtedly contribute substantive direction and additional inquiry to the development agenda for higher education to achieve the promise of community engagement.

References

Boyer, E. *Scholarship Reconsidered: Priorities of the Professoriate.* Princeton, N.J.: Carnegie Foundation for the Advancement of Teaching, 1990.
Boyer, E. "The Scholarship of Engagement." *Journal of Public Service and Outreach*, 1996, *1*(1), 11–20.
Driscoll, A. "Studying Faculty and Service-Learning: Directions for Inquiry and Development." *Michigan Journal of Community Service Learning*, Fall 2000, 35–41
Driscoll, A. "Carnegie's Community Engagement Classification: Intentions and Insights." *Change: The Magazine of Higher Learning*, 2008, *40*(1), 38–41.
O'Meara, K. A., and Rice, R. E. *Faculty Priorities Reconsidered: Rewarding Multiple Forms of Scholarship.* San Francisco: Jossey-Bass, 2005.
Zuiches, J. J., Cowling, E., Clark, J., Clayton, P., Helm, K., Henry, B., Morris, T., Moore, S., Navey-Davis, S., Schulze, S., Thornton, C., & Warren, A. "Attaining Carnegie's Community-Engagement Classification." *Change: The Magazine of Higher Learning*, 2008, *40*(1), 42–45.

AMY DRISCOLL *is a consulting scholar with the Carnegie Foundation for the Advancement of Teaching and coordinator for the community engagement classification.*

NEW DIRECTIONS FOR HIGHER EDUCATION • DOI: 10.1002/he

This chapter examines the characteristics and choices of leaders in Carnegie community-engaged classified institutions.

Leading the Engaged Institution

Lorilee R. Sandmann, William M. Plater

Leadership is a duty of presidents, provosts, and others responsible for the well-being of a college or university. The responsibilities of leadership are the subject of position descriptions and contracts, but the ways leaders enact these duties are matters of discretion. Leaders are differentiated by the choices they make.

In leading engaged institutions, executives can easily master the rhetoric of involvement and speak to audiences inside and outside the university with disarming conviction, but they must hold themselves accountable for the authenticity of their rhetoric and the alignment of consequence with declaration. There is no better way to test one's convictions than becoming attached to the local community—the neighborhood—through personal and direct interaction: conversation plus action. And the committed must determine whether the institutions they lead meet the criteria and judgment necessary for classification as an engaged campus.

Leading Questions

The elective Community Engagement Classification established by the Carnegie Foundation in 2006 highlights the role of leaders. One of the foundational indicators asks: "Does the executive leadership of the institution . . . explicitly promote community engagement as a priority?" Another asks, "Does the institution have a campus-wide coordinating infrastructure to support and

We acknowledge the assistance of University of Georgia doctoral graduate students Michael Massey and Anthony Omerikwa in the preparation of this chapter.

advance community engagement?" implying that opportunities for leadership may be dispersed across activity levels. Throughout the documentation framework, places exist where the role of individual leaders can be seen or inferred.

The roles of the chief executive officer (president or chancellor) and the chief academic officer (provost, vice chancellor, or dean of faculties) are distinct and critical because they stand as both the responsible and the symbolic leaders of the institution. They are the public and internal institutional faces, and their voices matter as indicators of sincerity in institutional commitment and identity formation. Sustained, deliberate, and unequivocal expression of the rationale for engagement—even if intermittent—counts for more than proclamations of convenience or opportunity. If even one of these leaders adopts a leadership style that suggests accommodation instead of transformation, others are excused from substantive engagement, and issues of leadership become more problematic.

In establishing the elective classification, Carnegie officials recognized the need for flexibility and breadth of interpretation of the meaning of community engagement. They acknowledged that mission statements must allow "institutional variations in philosophy, approaches, and contexts," as classification coordinator Amy Driscoll (2008, p. 39) explains in her commentary on the system. A standard template for documentation exists, but the forms, styles, and interpretations that responses can take are varied. Some will excel, and others will fall short. In all cases, there is an assumption that evidence will affirm proclamation. So it is with leading engaged institutions. There are contexts, approaches, philosophies, and styles for individual leaders, but the alignment of leadership with mission occurs as an individual choice, and the success of community engagement becomes a reflection of personal engagement, including measurable results to back up claims.

Close and Direct Leadership

John Dewey articulated a principle in *The Public and Its Problems* that continues to underlie the rationale for university involvement in communities and their responsibility for graduating competent citizens: "In its deepest and richest sense a community must always remain a matter of face-to-face intercourse. . . . There is no substitute for the vitality and depth of close and direct intercourse and attachment. . . . Democracy must begin at home and its home is the neighborly community" (Coughlan, 1975, pp. 97, 98).

What matters most to understanding the role leaders play in giving life to mission and institutional purpose is the idea of "close and direct intercourse and attachment." Leaders must be personally involved if management and administration are to give way to vision, transformation, and inspiration. Without attachment and sincere commitment, leadership dissembles.

Leaders are trendsetters, role models, and exemplars. If they are seen to be engaged rhetorically but absent personally, then a pattern of superficiality is established. Presidents and provosts are especially suspect because of their tendency to espouse new ideas and challenges at each fall faculty convocation. No matter how global the aspirations of leadership, engagement is always hollowed out and transient without the product of direct intercourse and attachment, when engagement does not begin in the campus neighborhood, and when dialogue is not routinely face-to-face. The wise president or provost will be intentional about associations with community leaders, thoughtfully seeking several highly visible occasions throughout the year to appear in person on and off campus in the presence of a public figure recognized by the community and institution alike as a dedicated steward of place.

When leaders are engaged and their actions match their rhetoric, their influence grows in accordance with the length of their involvement and the public nature of their participation. At a time when community has attained the fluidity of convenience as we belong to multiple communities that are global, disciplinary, transcendent, and, increasingly, electronic, other administrators, faculty, staff, students, and trustees long for the certainty of belonging to a physical community even as they want it to be international in its connections. When university and community leaders know and trust each other, their association inspires others to make a similar investment in counterparts at all levels of leadership.

By engaging themselves, leaders engage their whole institution. The reverse is not possible, even when the tradition of engagement is strong. A new leader who is not personally engaged will discover that decades of involvement can be forgotten in months of indifference. Practicing leadership is an exercise in symbolic action, and leaders who understand and accept this role are more likely to succeed than those who do not.

We have come to appreciate that engaged leadership has four stages: (1) interpreting institutional mission to reflect engagement with multiple communities beginning with the local geographical community, (2) defining specific objectives and goals to implement the mission, (3) articulating the means and priorities for taking action to achieve the goals, and (4) manifesting commitment through personal interaction—face-to-face, as Dewey says.

Other steps to consider are resource allocation, planning, and personnel policies, but these are secondary to the personal engagement of leaders at the executive, classroom, or student level. While only two years old, the Carnegie classification of community-engaged institutions reveals noteworthy patterns of leadership.

Characteristics of Institutions Leading the Engagement Movement

Generally the patterns of the institutions leading the engagement movement, and in particular their leaders and the structures they have implemented to facilitate their engagement efforts, were identified by analyzing responses to questions II.A.5 on communication by executive leadership

NEW DIRECTIONS FOR HIGHER EDUCATION • DOI: 10.1002/he

and II.B.1 on supporting infrastructures of the Carnegie Community Engagement Classification framework. Specifically the questions are: (II.A.5) Does the executive leadership (President, Provost, Chancellor, Trustees, etc.) of the institution communicate explicitly to promote community engagement as a priority? Yes / No; Describe, quote; (II.B.1) Does the college have a coordinating infrastructure (center, office, etc.) to support and advance community engagement? Yes / No; Describe with purposes, staffing (Carnegie Foundation for the Advancement of Teaching, 2007, 2008). These questions were analyzed from the documentation of fifty-six of the seventy-six successful Carnegie applications. Of those, fifty-three were four-year colleges or universities, and three were two-year public colleges. Nine were private, nonprofit institutions; the others were public. These institutions clustered in the eastern and midwestern United States, and California had six institutions so classified. One was classified as curricular engaged, six as outreach and partnerships, and the remaining forty-nine achieved classification in both curricular engagement and outreach and partnerships.

Review of the data revealed a wide range of commitment, implementation, and operating scale. Using the constant-comparative qualitative method (Ruona, 2005), we identified the themes that serve as the primary basis for discussion in this chapter, although we draw on corroborating findings from other sources as well.

Defining the Leader's Role

This section discusses characteristics of those leading these Carnegie community-engaged institutions. It was found that position and passion play key roles.

Executive Leadership. Engagement is leadership driven and stakeholder focused. Initially engagement was led by faculty champions, civic-minded students, and strident community partners. However, now stakeholder numbers are increasing, especially among institutions' executive leadership. The classification documentation indicates that leadership is multilayered, and executive leadership, consisting of chancellors, presidents, and provosts, is the dominant layer. The difference between the functions and stakeholders of the leader groups, with presidents using rhetoric as their primary tool to communicate the importance of engagement, is discernable. Ample evidence exists of presidents and chancellors showing leadership by interpreting the institutional mission to reflect engagement with multiple communities and defining specific objectives to implement that mission. In contrast, provosts were proactive internally and articulated priorities to interpret engagement within the mission, particularly as related to student impact. Limited examples of presidents and provosts sharing commitment through personal interaction arose. An exception was John D. Welty, president of California State University–Fresno, who called on the campus to join him to work to improve literacy rates. He announced the university's involvement in a K-3 tutoring program, ReadFresno, and he and every staff member in his office joined the program as tutors.

In addition to internal executive leadership, others play critical roles. Often engagement leadership has an appointed engagement designee with titles such as vice president for university engagement (University of Kentucky), vice president for regional development (Kent State University), vice president for outreach and international affairs (Virginia Tech), assistant to the president for community engagement and diversity issues (Widener University), and associate provost for community engagement (University of Baltimore).

Some institutions have operational leaders, such as director of the center for public and community service (Syracuse University) or coordinator for the Office for Service Learning and Community Outreach (OSLCO) (University of Massachusetts Boston). The latter serves "as a resource to community partners, faculty, students, and staff to enhance civic participation and promote community-based learning opportunities."

When engagement is aligned as an institution-wide priority, evidence of leadership resides in the portfolios of senior campus leaders. At the University of Kentucky, for example, the vice president for university engagement has a staff of thirty full- and part-time employees, and the university's cooperative extension has a thousand employees. The university's vice president for institutional advancement also supports the work, and several of its academic colleges have positions devoted to engagement.

Personal Mission. Beyond formal expectations of their positions and mission, leaders may hold the values of engagement as a personal mission. They seek institutions whose missions are aligned with their own or carry their dedication from post to post. Chancellor Nancy Cantor came to Syracuse University from the University of Illinois at Urbana-Champaign, where she was chancellor, and the University of Michigan, where she was provost and executive vice president for academic affairs. Cantor has been an advocate for racial justice, diversity, and community engagement, so it was not surprising that she went on to promote scholarship in action as one of Syracuse University's guiding principles. Likewise, Judith Ramaley, a three-time president, brought her passion and commitment to civic and community engagement to Winona State University.

During the interview process for president of Widener University, James T. Harris III was explicit about his intention to make civic engagement a cornerstone of his administration. He launched the first formal strategic planning process in Widener's history and signaled his commitment by creating a special assistant to the president for community engagement. He appointed the civic engagement committee to provide oversight to motivate students to engage in issues of social responsibility and set their paths toward shaping a more inclusive, just, and compassionate world.

New Directions for Higher Education • DOI: 10.1002/he

Another example is Elizabeth D. Capaldi, who became executive vice president and provost of Arizona State University in 2006. She was attracted to the university because it articulates and acts on its commitment to connect academic work and the community.

Leadership to Advance Engagement

Evidence of how these leaders of engaged institutions perform the tasks of leadership is illustrated by three aspects of the documentation provided for Carnegie Community Engagement Classification: leaders' messages in public presentations, planning documents, and structures implemented to support, advance, and execute community engagement. All three tasks lend substance to the symbolic and public engagement of academic leaders with their community counterparts.

Messages of Presidents and Provosts. Our findings of how individual leaders conceptualize and frame engagement are similar to those of Ronning, Keeney, and Sanford (2008), who analyzed the language and themes of forty-five presidential speeches. These presidents, they wrote, are "symbolic manifestations of the possibility that state universities promise their citizens" (p. 5). Regardless of the audience, they found that all presidents discussed "(1) accomplishments of their institutions; (2) the contract between the institutions and state or community; (3) challenges within the context of higher education; and (4) economic development potential of academic institutions" (p. 5). Similarly, we found for the Carnegie institutions a range of purpose underlying engagement, but the most prominent themes were contributions to economic and workforce development, responding to social needs, and producing citizens of character. Two brief excerpts, taken from their respective institution's applications, illustrate these themes:

- University of Memphis president Shirley Raines says, "We want to build the most productive partnerships in which nonprofits, industry, government agencies and communities get something from us and we in turn get something from them."
- Western Kentucky University's president, Gary Ransdell, remarks, "My comments this morning [opening address to faculty and staff in 2007 academic year] would be incomplete if I did not acknowledge the nature of our 'publicness' as a state university and an important agency of state government. . . . We are proud of our publicness and our responsibility to be a good steward of this region even while our mission is rapidly changing in dramatic ways."

A more comprehensive example of the power of presidential messages comes from Tufts University president Lawrence S. Bacow, a lawyer and economist whose research focuses on environmental polity. Although each of his messages is adapted to its intended audience, all reflect a consistent expression of ideas. His 2003 presentation, "Tufts: A University Poised," focused on the Tisch College of Citizenship and Public Service, which provides education geared toward active citizenship. In 2005, he said in "How Universities Can Teach Public Service," as reported in Tufts' Carnegie application, "As caught up as we all get in the demands of our daily lives, we can find the time and the resources to do something for the greater good of our community, our nation, and the world. . . . I believe we need to make civic engagement the norm, not the exception."

In his annual matriculation speeches, President Bacow emphasizes the importance of active citizenship to each class of incoming first-year students. Again, reported in the Tufts' application, he told the class of 2009, "We still believe that education and the generation of new knowledge are fundamental to a free and just society. And we believe that with education comes responsibility, responsibility to make the world a better place. At Tufts, we embrace active citizenship as one of our core values." And when Bacow testified before the Secretary of Education's Commission on the Future of Higher Education, he asserted, "Our institutions should be motivating students to become active, engaged and effective citizens in the communities they will inhabit. This is the role of a liberal education, not just to convey knowledge, but to convey values also, to encourage our students to get involved and not sit on the sidelines." When leaders become self-aware and intentional about their influence, they can—as these exemplars do—review the texts of speeches, messages, and Web site greetings to ensure that the language of engagement reflects the level of their personal commitment.

Setting Institutional Direction. Leaders use a strategic planning process to drive the institutionalization of engagement. For instance, Kent State University's strategic plan served as a transition guide between presidents and ensured the sustainability of its engagement ethos. Its five-year plan for the years 2004 to 2009 is widely referenced and promotes institutional goals that include principles such as "engage with the world beyond our campuses" and "build and sustain relationships that foster success."

Strategic planning processes have been used to provide a mechanism for other groups to exert leadership as well. An example is the University of St. Thomas board of trustees, which passed a statement of priorities that reiterates the core commitments of engagement. In 2003 the Rhodes College board of trustees adopted a vision statement, which is printed on a card for every member of the Rhodes community, promoting community engagement that is translated into college initiatives: student services reengineering to improve the effectiveness of student services; the Crossroads to Freedom Project, a digital archive of civil rights–era artifacts from Memphis; and the Center for Academic Research and Education Through Service to involve students in research and service.

From president to trustees, from deans to provost, leaders who have a duty to set institutional direction can ensure a prominent place for engagement by calling on everyone to include an assessment of their personal involvement in their annual performance reports. The occasion for an annual reflection on goals is the best way to ensure that the institution continues to be pointed in the right direction.

Organizational Structures to Support Engagement. In addition to executive messages and institutional direction setting, leaders advance an engagement agenda through organization and allocation of resources. These leaders have established a variety of organizational structures, staff, and reporting relationships. Three types of infrastructure support engagement: centralized centers, diffused networks, and a hybrid model of complex, targeted, yet diffused units. Leadership occurs in three divisions: academic affairs, public or government relations or institutional advancement, and student affairs. Coordination among these divisions is achieved at two levels: the board and executive staff level and committees that include faculty, staff, students, and, in a few cases, community partners. Most units report to the provost or a senior vice president; in smaller institutions, units report to the president. Few units are located in student affairs.

Coordinating Centralized Centers. A typical organizational structure is a center. Bates College's Harward Center for Community Partnerships, for example, leads Bates's efforts in community involvement and community-based education and builds on existing programs in service-learning, community volunteerism, and environmental stewardship. The center's mission is to collaborate with community partners to meet community needs and integrate civic engagement. A director leads the center and reports to the president. Another example is Indiana State University's Center for Public Service and Community Engagement, which serves as a front door to university resources. The center coordinates the outreach mission and community engagement, including service-learning, economic development, and community-based research. The center director reports to the provost.

The Leo T. McCarthy Center for Public Service and the Common Good at the University of San Francisco exemplifies units that provide direct support to academic units. It offers a public service certificate program and an honors public service academic minor. It links more than two hundred community, state, national, and international agencies to six schools and colleges, the university ministry, and the Division of University Life for Community Engagement. The center, staffed by the director, assistant director, and student assistants, supports academic programs and research projects and provides students with service-learning and intern opportunities. It also sponsors projects that involve students in faculty-led ventures, such as sponsoring speakers, panel presentations, and other forums that expose students to the community,

Another common practice is redefining or expanding existing units. When Virginia Commonwealth University's strategic plan called for restructuring, it reorganized and renamed the Office of Community Programs as the

Division of Community Engagement, and the director position was elevated to vice provost, reporting to the provost and vice president for academic affairs.

Diffused Networked Units. Some institutions use a decentralized, diffused approach. At Arizona State University's Tempe Campus, engagement is realized through multiple centers, colleges, and departments with staffing and facilities responsive to the needs of interdisciplinary programs. This organic infrastructure interconnects across the university in relational networks. Each networked unit takes ownership for community-based initiatives. Sharing of information and best practices is facilitated through monthly meetings of the Outreach Initiatives Committee.

Hybrid Coordinated Networks. Syracuse University coordinates engagement at the highest level of administration through the three Offices of Academic Affairs, Government and Community Relations, and Institutional Advancement. Cabinet-level accountability ensures that leadership for engagement is a top priority. The associate vice president of the Office of Engagement Initiatives reports to the senior vice president of institutional advancement, who reports to the chancellor. The office has six staff members and an operating budget of $1 million with a mission to implement the university's vision through specific programs and initiatives that leverage the support and engagement of alumni, friends, government, and other institution supporters. The office provides direction, strategic planning, and resolution as it implements targeted community engagement programs locally, nationally, and globally. Office staff members also act as liaisons or ombudspersons between the chancellor's office and the community.

This type of unit can occur at smaller, highly evolved, engaged universities such as the University of St. Thomas, where offices coordinate undergraduate service-learning and community engagement and provide a link to the institution's eight schools and colleges. The Center for Community Partnerships provides a single entry point and source of information for students, faculty, and staff to partner with the community.

Deeper Reflections on Leadership

Successful institutions manifest extensive involvement of executive leadership that speaks consistently about the engagement mission and embeds it in institutional planning. In all cases, institutional structures reflect specific line authority and accountability for engagement. Leadership titles, organizational structures, and resource and funding mechanisms vary as progress is achieved.

Applicant responses to the two questions in the Carnegie framework on leadership and structure are rich and provide an inventory of significant and promising practices that offer the potential for emulation at other interested postsecondary institutions. It is noteworthy, however, that three themes have emerged with insufficient commentary or analysis as yet to identify them as important trends for leadership:

1. Although leaders often communicate the economic development impacts of engagement, they do not discuss the impact of engagement on such social change or public policy variables as access, efficiency, equity, and participation. Perhaps this represents the bias of those who completed the Carnegie applications, but it offers an opportunity for public policy research.
2. Despite leaders' inclusion of engagement in strategic planning and demands for accountability in higher education, there is virtually no linkage of engagement with evaluation, outcomes, or accreditation of postsecondary education.
3. Engagement programs exist at local and regional levels. Mention of national and international programs is limited in the communications of leaders to their stakeholders (most of whom are arguably local or regional), although the proliferation of global social issues is evident.

Much can be learned in subsequent classification rounds about what these omissions mean in regard to engaged leadership. Questions arise, such as: Who among leaders is more determinant in an institution's engagement? How necessary are personal commitment and visible personal engagement— and for how long? How do leaders advance engagement beyond their own terms in office? Indeed, in the future it may be important to consider leadership beyond the individuals whose offices and titles confer both duty and choice. What are the forms of collective leadership that exist inherently in organizational structures? A starting point would be to map the key processes and activities of engagement to see if there are critical but unacknowledged leaders.

Leadership Challenges

Leadership is not easy, it is never formulaic, and it is always personal. Successful adopters demonstrate multiple ways to define and engage communities, but a common denominator is the threshold level of committed leadership.

The institution must not only promote community engagement but must also manifest an alignment of commitment, mission, public declaration, resources, policies and procedures (including recognition of civic engagement as proper faculty work), planning, measurable goals, and accountability. While presidents or provosts cannot—and should not—preside personally over these vital functions, their alignment will not occur without personal leadership.

Effective leadership is dispersed without losing coherence or the focus of shared purpose. Whether assigned or assumed, leadership depends on a consistent commitment from higher levels. Each level needs to inform, inspire, and transform with direct intercourse and attachment within the academy and the community.

Truly engaged universities have leaders in many roles, all of whom can interact with a shared commitment because they are also personal commitments. No president engages a community by herself and no provost decides faculty acceptance by himself, but together they define a style of engagement that leads the whole institution.

While community engagement must derive from mission instead of the president or provost's ambitions, one of the most vexing challenges is ensuring continuity as key leaders depart. The turnover frequency averages between five and seven years, so leaders must ensure sustainability by articulating engagement as a function of mission and appointing leaders who share a personal commitment. Perhaps none is more critical to sustainability than the person responsible for coordinating infrastructure to support and advance community engagement. Through this intermediary, the leading officers can oversee faculty involvement and buy-in, as well as provide an accountable framework for direct community participation.

Habits of Leadership

Leadership performs indispensable roles at all levels. In its cumulative impact, leadership shapes institutional behavior and practices—what John Dewey called "habits of living." In fact, individual colleges and universities can themselves be considered institutional leaders: a culture and ethos emerge from the shared vision and commitment of the leaders at all levels—people who reflect community engagement as a habit of living. Such commitment needs to be made formal and celebrated through mission statements and public declarations, but community engagement will endure only when the belief, the commitment, and the actions are so pervasive—so habitual—that their withdrawal would be painful. At that point, community engagement, through effective leadership, has become institutionalized.

References

Carnegie Foundation for the Advancement of Teaching. "Elective Classification: Community Engagement—2008 Documentation Framework." 2007. Retrieved June 29, 2009, from http://www.carnegiefoundation.org/dynamic/downloads/file_1_614.pdf.

Carnegie Foundation for the Advancement of Teaching. "Community Engagement." Retrieved June 29, 2009, from http://www.carnegiefoundation.org/classifications/index.asp?key=1213.

Coughlan, N. Young John Dewey: An Essay in American Intellectual History. Chicago: University of Chicago Press, 1975.

Driscoll, A. "Carnegie's Community-Engagement Classification: Intentions and Insights." *Change: The Magazine of Higher Learning*, 2008, *40*(1) 38–41.

Ronning, E. A., Keeney, B. E., and Sanford, T. "Advocating for the Public Good: A Study of Presidential Communication." Paper presented at the American Education Research Association Annual Meeting, New York, 2008.

Ruona, W. E. A. "Analyzing Qualitative Data." In R. A. Swanson and E. F. Holton III (eds.), *Research in Organizations: Foundations and Methods of Inquiry*. San Francisco: Berrett-Koehler, 2005.

LORILEE R. SANDMANN *is associate professor in the Department of Lifelong Learning, Administration, and Policy at the University of Georgia and director of the National Review Board for the Scholarship of Engagement.*

WILLIAM M. PLATER *is Chancellor's Professor of Public Affairs, Philanthropic Studies, English, and Informatics at Indiana University–Purdue University Indianapolis.*

NEW DIRECTIONS FOR HIGHER EDUCATION • DOI: 10.1002/he

3

Community-engaged colleges and universities are revising promotion and tenure policies to reward community-engaged scholarship.

Rewarding Community-Engaged Scholarship

John Saltmarsh, Dwight E. Giles Jr., Elaine Ward, Suzanne M. Buglione

Faculty members, in their roles as arbiters of the curriculum, teachers, knowledge producers, and citizens, hold a prominent role in realizing the goal of making higher education more responsive to community and public welfare. For faculty to claim, own, and foster institutional efforts to connect the campus more meaningfully with society calls for reward structures that clearly define and reward this type of work.

—K. Ward (2005)

Higher education leaders seeking to reshape institutional identity and establish community engagement as a core institutional value ultimately have to address how to embed the values of community engagement in the institutional reward policies that define the faculty roles of teaching, scholarship, and service (Lynton, 1995; Driscoll and Lynton, 1999; O'Meara, 2000, 2002, 2003; Ward, 2003, 2005; Ellison and Eatman, 2008). Furthermore, since the research university culture dominates the construction of faculty roles in higher education, community engagement must be recognized explicitly in the criteria for scholarly work if it is to reshape faculty culture. It cannot be relegated to either the faculty's teaching or service roles exclusively, but must be included as part of the faculty's scholarship and research role (Weerts and Sandmann, 2008).

We acknowledge Deborah Milbauer, consultant from CommunityBuild, for her valuable research assistance. We also thank the Graduate College of Education at the University of Massachusetts Boston for providing graduate assistantships to support this study.

While the extent to which community-engaged scholarship is part of the research agenda of any given faculty member is shaped by "the type of institution, as well as the individual goals of the faculty member" (Ward, 2005, p. 224), campuses that want to create a culture supporting community-engaged faculty work, Ward explains, "must define in their promotion and tenure guidelines and faculty handbooks what this work looks like, and how it will be evaluated and rewarded" (p. 229). "No matter how clear the mission statement or presidential proclamation to connect the campus with the community," observes Ward, if community engagement is "unrewarded or seen by faculty as distracting from the pursuit of those kinds of things that count on a dossier, either those public service efforts will be set aside, or the faculty member will be. Either way community approaches to scholarship will not be strengthened" (p. 228).

Faculty scholarly work and its reward provide the context for the questions related to institutional reward policies that appear in the "optional questions" section of foundational indicators of the 2006 Carnegie community engagement framework. The questions on institutional reward policies are aimed at three aspects of rewarding community-engaged scholarship: what exists in current policy, which of the faculty roles are rewarded for community engagement, and if changes in the promotion and tenure guidelines to reward community-engaged scholarship have not been implemented, whether a process is under way to revise the current guidelines.

This chapter presents findings that are part of a larger qualitative study of the applications, faculty handbooks, and key informant interviews from Carnegie community-engaged campuses. For the purposes of this study, we focused on campuses that emerged as the most engaged: those that received the classification for curricular engagement and for outreach and partnerships. We surmised that these campuses would be more likely to have community engagement articulated in the institutional reward policies. Of the sixty-two campuses that received the classification for curricular engagement and for outreach and partnerships, thirty-three elected to answer the question on reward policies and provided documentation to support their answer. For five of the campuses, we were unable to gain permission to use the application for this study. Eight campuses from Carnegie's 2005 pilot cohort for the classification are also included in the final sample. Finally, it should be noted that of the thirty-three campuses that answered yes to the question of whether the institution has policies that reward the scholarship of engagement, two of the institutions do not grant tenure.

What It Means to Reward Community-Engaged Scholarship

Our study of the Carnegie applications begins with a framing of what it means to reward community-engaged scholarship in the light of two key considerations: community partner relations and change in institutional culture.

NEW DIRECTIONS FOR HIGHER EDUCATION • DOI: 10.1002/he

Characteristics of the relationship between campus and community have an impact on policy formation, and changes in institutional reward policies for faculty are emblematic of changes in institutional culture and institutional identity.

Community Partner Relations. The 2006 elective Community Engagement Classification defines community engagement as "the collaboration between higher education institutions and their larger communities (local, regional/state, national, global) for the mutually beneficial exchange of knowledge and resources in a context of partnership and reciprocity." The quality of this engagement is defined such that engagement is equated with reciprocity. Reciprocity specifically signals a shift in campus-community partnerships toward relationships that are defined by a multidirectional flow of knowledge and expertise between campus and community in collaborative efforts to address community-based issues.

In *Scholarship Reconsidered* (1990), Boyer identified one of four areas of scholarship as the "scholarship of application," which "moves toward engagement as the scholar asks, 'How can knowledge be responsibly applied to consequential problems?'" (p. 21). By 1996, Boyer emphasized higher education's "civic mandate" (1990, p. 16) more forcefully than he had in *Scholarship Reconsidered* across all forms of scholarship with what he called the "scholarship of engagement." One characteristic of the scholarship of engagement, according to Boyer, is that it "means creating a special climate in which the academic and civic cultures communicate more continuously and more creatively with each other . . . enriching the quality of life for us all" (p. 20). That special climate is explicitly and intentionally inclusive, collaborative, and problem oriented, and it is one in which academics share knowledge-generating tasks with the public and involve community partners as participants in public problem solving.

Since Boyer's writings, scholars have drawn distinctions between the scholarship of application and the scholarship of engagement. The scholarship of application, write O'Meara and Rice, "builds on established academic epistemology, assumes that knowledge is generated in the university or college and then applied to external contexts with knowledge flowing in one direction, out of the academy." The scholarship of engagement, in contrast, is based on reciprocity and

> requires going beyond the expert model that often gets in the way of constructive university-community collaboration . . . calls on faculty to move beyond "outreach," . . . asks scholars to go beyond "service," with its overtones of noblesse oblige. What it emphasizes is genuine *collaboration*: that the learning and teaching be multidirectional and the expertise shared. It represents a basic reconceptualization of faculty involvement in community-based work [p. 28].

The framework the Carnegie Foundation provides for community engagement is shaped by this reconceptualization and views community-engaged

New Directions for Higher Education • DOI: 10.1002/he

scholarship as grounded in community partnership relations defined by reciprocity.

Reciprocity also implies that community-engaged scholarship is assessed differently than traditional scholarship is. Glassick, Huber, and Maeroff (1997) make the point in *Scholarship Assessed* that new forms of scholarship are "not always a peer-reviewed article or book" (p. 38). Community-engaged scholarship redefines what constitutes a "publication" and redefines who is a "peer" in the peer review process.

Changes in Institutional Culture and Identity. In their 1998 study of institutional culture and change in higher education, Eckel, Hill, and Green describe changes that "alter the culture of the institution" as those that require "major shifts in an institution's culture—the common set of beliefs and values that creates a shared interpretation and understanding of events and actions" (p. 3). It is the elements of institutional culture and identity that constitute the foundational indicators section of the community engagement framework. Central to the question of changing institutional culture is redefining faculty promotion and tenure guidelines.

Eckel, Hill, and Green conclude that efforts being made in higher education around "connecting institutions to their communities" offer the potential for fundamentally changing institutional identity. This could occur, they write, because "these connections can contribute to the reshaping of institutional practices and purposes . . . [Campuses] may reconsider the types of service rewarded through merit pay and promotion and tenure policies, and they may adopt wider definitions of scholarship" (p. 7).

Change in institutional identity occurs when shifts in the institution's culture have developed to the point where it is both pervasive across the institution and deeply embedded in practices throughout the institution. Analysis of the applications allowed us to better understand not only how community-engaged scholarship is being recognized in promotion and tenure policies, but also the degree to which changes in policies suggest change in institutional culture.

How Community-Engaged Scholarship Is Being Rewarded

Analysis of the applications indicates the emergence of significant revision of institutional polices that rewards faculty for community-engaged scholarship. This emerging change has a number of dimensions. First, it is change that takes place over time; thus, there is a transitional quality to what is happening on campuses as they engage in a process of defining, implementing, and adjusting to the implications of change. These are campuses where institutional reward policies are in a process of transition to rewarding community-engaged scholarship. Many more campuses are involved in the difficult and often long process of revising their promotion and tenure guidelines than there are campuses that have already revised and adopted new policies. For those that have revised their promotion and tenure guidelines to reward community-engaged scholarship, the policies exhibit a quality of establishing conceptual clarity around community engagement, address engagement across the faculty roles, and are grounded in reciprocity.

Policies in a Process of Transition. Nearly half of the campuses studied are in the process of revising their promotion and tenure policies. It was not uncommon to have a campus explain in its application, as this one did, that "at the institutional level, we are currently moving to revise Faculty Handbook tenure and promotion guidelines to reflect the importance of community engagement as a scholarly activity" and that "all departments have been asked to review tenure and promotion guidelines to ensure that engagement of students with community is part of the expectations for faculty."

The range of policy revision processes reveals a continuum. On one end of the continuum is new presidential leadership that pronounces a new vision for the campus and initiates a process of reexamining the academic culture around engagement but has not yet effected a change in policies. Along the continuum, campuses indicate an ongoing process with faculty committees involved in making recommendations to change criteria for promotion and tenure, and in some cases evidence reveals that some, if not all, of the proposed changes have been adopted in revised policies. On the other end of the continuum is evidence of campuses with fully revised promotion and tenure guidelines that incorporate specific criteria for community-engaged scholarship. The examples that we provide illustrate actual changes in campus promotion and tenure guidelines, not aspirations for policy revisions.

Most prominent in the revision process is the adoption of guidelines that broaden scholarly activity in Boyer's four realms: the scholarship of discovery, the scholarship of integration, the scholarship of teaching, and the scholarship of application. As this adoption represents a transitional movement toward rewarding community-engaged scholarship, community engagement is less specifically written into policies than it is implied in their interpretation. For example, one campus explained its use of Boyer's categories of scholarship in this way:

> The Scholarship category is broadly defined as "Scholarship and Related Professional Activities," and Boyer's four types of scholarship (discovery, integration, application, teaching) are made explicit. Given these broad definitions, faculty scholarship related to community engagement is rewarded in promotion and tenure decision . . . The point is that our scholarship criteria are broadly defined and community engagement activities are regularly key components of scholarship in successful P&T application . . . Community engagement scholarship fits logically as scholarship of integration, application or teaching.

NEW DIRECTIONS FOR HIGHER EDUCATION • DOI: 10.1002/he

As this example indicates, community-engaged scholarship "logically," but without explanation, could be evaluated under integration, application, or teaching. In some cases, the campus application noted that "we don't fit the community engagement scholarship into one of Boyer's other categories; we recognize that engagement can cross-cut them all."

More common was to have community-engaged scholarship specifically subsumed under the scholarship of application:

> The Faculty Handbook uses the term "scholarship of application" in its standards for promotion and tenure. Summarizing Boyer, the handbook states, "This involves applying disciplinary expertise to the exploration or solution of individual, social, or institutional problems; it involves activities that are tied directly to one's special field of knowledge and it demands the same level of rigor and accountability as is traditionally associated with research activities."

Occasionally "application" referred specifically to community-related interactions, as in "scholarship encompasses . . . the application of knowledge in responsible ways to consequential problems of contemporary society, the larger community, so that one's scholarly specialty informs and is informed by interactions with that community." More often "application" was used as a broad category into which community engagement activity most logically fit: "Application involves asking how state-of-the-art knowledge can be responsibly applied to significant problems. Application primarily concerns assessing the efficacy of knowledge or creative activities within a particular context, refining its implications, assessing its generalizability, and using it to implement changes."

Most of the campuses employing Boyer's categories do so in ways that include a broader view of scholarly activity but maintain a traditional approach to evaluation through academic peer-reviewed publications as in the following example: "Scholarship of Application: This involves applying disciplinary expertise to the exploration or solution of individual, social, or institutional problems; it involves activities that are tied directly to one's special field of knowledge and it demands the same level of rigor and accountability as is traditionally associated with research activities." This formulation suggests that community-engaged scholarship must adhere to the criteria of traditional scholarship as judged by publication in disciplinary, peer-reviewed journals.

Conceptual Clarity. Campuses that have revised their promotion and tenure guidelines to explicitly reward the scholarship of community engagement tend to be clear and consistent in the use of terminology that reinforces engaged faculty work. When the reward of engaged scholarship is implied or unstated or when it is used to reward engagement as a service activity or in relation to teaching, the terminology used shapes the characteristics of engagement. Table 3.1 shows the wide variation in the language used to convey engagement activity. (For further discussion of language differences and the evolution of civic engagement terminology, see Sandmann, 2008, and Giles, 2008.)

Table 3.1 Engagement Terms and Frequency of Use in the Carnegie Applications

Term	Number of Times Used
Service to the Community/Public	10
Service-Learning	8
Community Engagement	7
Application-from Boyer	6
Outreach/Engagement (Extension)	5
Engaged Scholarship	2
Civic Engagement	2
Scholarship of Community Engagement	2
Scholarship Related to Public Engagement Mission	2
Community-Based Research	1
Scholarly Civic Engagement	1
Service-Related Publications	1
Scholarship Which Enhances Public Good	1
Civic Engagement Scholarship	1

Note: The terminology varied within and across institutions.

Regardless of the unique institutional culture that shapes the framework of engagement on a campus, clear policy formulation rewarding the scholarship of community engagement corresponds with concrete definition of scholarly engagement. For example, one campus explicitly identifies engagement as "the partnership of university knowledge and resources with those of the public and private sectors to enrich scholarship, research, and creative activity; enhance curriculum, teaching and learning; prepare educated, engaged citizens; strengthen democratic values and civic responsibility; address critical societal issues; and contribute to the public good."

As it continued to revise its tenure and promotion policies, another campus formulated a working definition of *engaged scholarship* as

> scholarship that 1) engages faculty members and students in a collaborative and sustained manner with urban, regional, state, national and/or global communities; 2) conceptualizes "community groups" as all those outside of academe; (3) requires shared authority at all stages of the research process from defining the research problem, choosing theoretical and methodological approaches, conducting the research, developing the final product(s), to participating in peer evaluation; and 4) results in products such as conventional peer reviewed publications, collaborative reports, documentation of impact, and continuing external funding.

With this clarity of definition, the academic leadership encourages departments "to refine the definition as appropriate for diverse disciplines and to develop guidelines for evaluating such scholarship for the purposes

NEW DIRECTIONS FOR HIGHER EDUCATION • DOI: 10.1002/he

of tenure and promotion." The importance of clarity of definition reinforces Ward's findings (2005) and provides the basis for establishing criteria for evaluating community-engaged scholarship across the disciplines.

Engagement Across Faculty Roles. Our analysis confirms what Amy Driscoll observes of the 2006 applicants: that "most institutions continue to place community engagement and its scholarship in the traditional category of service and require other forms of scholarship for promotion and tenure" (2008, p. 41). Yet the applications also reveal examples of scholarly engagement across the faculty roles, especially when there is conceptual clarity and when scholarly engagement is clearly defined and delineated as scholarly work. One campus's policies state that "the University's strong commitment to public engagement may be reflected in any or all of these categories [teaching, research, and service]. Public engagement is defined as discipline-related collaborations between faculty members and communities, agencies, organizations, businesses, governments, or the general public that contribute significantly to the external constituency by sharing the University's intellectual and cultural assets." The way community engagement is defined determines its place in the work of faculty.

Ward (2005) notes that "the scholarship of engagement . . . is by definition integrated, and most promotion and tenure guidelines are compartmentalized" (p. 229). For one campus, the promotion and tenure guidelines state that "one should recognize that research, teaching, and community outreach often overlap. For example, a service learning project may reflect both teaching and community outreach. Some research projects may involve both research and community outreach. Pedagogical research may involve both research and teaching." At another campus, "a faculty member's community engagement activities may be defined and recognized by X College's faculty committee . . . in any of the three categories of expected and assessed performance for tenure-track and tenured faculty: 1) research/scholarship, 2) teaching, and/or 3) service. The Committee . . . is likely to recognize a faculty member's community engagement work as scholarship when it is part of his/her record of research and publication, as teaching when it involves [theory-practice] courses or community engagement or is part of a partnership or community project that enhances the College's service profile." These examples convey not only the seamlessness and integration across faculty roles but also a clear articulation of how community engagement is rewarded across all areas of faculty work.

Reciprocity. One of the significant challenges that emerged from the 2006 applications was in the area of establishing reciprocal campus-community relationships. As Driscoll (2008) reports, "Most institutions could only describe in vague generalities how they had achieved genuine reciprocity with their communities" (p. 41). This observation is consistent with our analysis. The discourse around community engagement that is done "to" or "in" the community is contrasted with applications that expressed collaborative, multidirectional relationships that define reciprocity.

New Directions for Higher Education • DOI: 10.1002/he

One application indicates awareness of the distinction between engagement "in" the community and engagement "with" the community by "distinguishing between (a) community engagement, which is defined solely by the location of the activity (e.g., teaching, research, and service in the community), and (b) civic engagement, which is defined as teaching, research, and service that is both in and *with* the community." For another campus, reciprocity is found in policy documents that codify "accomplishments in extension and engagement [as] *an ongoing two-way interchange of knowledge, information, understanding, and services* between the university and the state, nation, and world."

Campuses that adopted Boyer's categories tended to frame community engagement as "application to" a community instead of engagement "with." Reciprocity was clearly apparent when a distinction was made between the scholarship of application and the scholarship of engagement, as well as a distinction made between partnership and reciprocity:

> Engaged scholarship now subsumes the scholarship of application. It adds to existing knowledge in the process of applying intellectual expertise to collaborative problem-solving with urban, regional, state, national and/or global communities and results in a written work shared with others in the discipline or field of study. Engaged scholarship conceptualizes "community groups" as all those outside of academe and requires shared authority at all stages of the research process from defining the research problem, choosing theoretical and methodological approaches, conducting the research, developing the final product(s), to participating in peer evaluation.

This conceptualization of reciprocity implies that community-engaged scholarship is assessed differently from traditional scholarship. It redefines what constitutes a "publication" and redefines who is a "peer" in the peer review process. Other applications, although not as comprehensive, express some elements of reciprocity; one includes criteria for publications that specify "reports, including technical reports, reports prepared for a community partner or to be submitted by a community partner." In another, evidence of high-quality scholarship can be demonstrated through "letters from external colleagues, external agencies, or organizations attesting to the quality and value of the work." In both cases, reciprocity as an underlying value of engagement is potentially changing the institutional culture of the campus.

The Future of Engaged Scholarship

For administrators and faculty who seek to create a supportive academic culture in which community-engaged scholarship can thrive, the evidence from the 2006 Carnegie Community Engagement Classification applications can provide useful guidance. Evidence from the applications indicates that shifting an institutional commitment to community engagement is an enormously

NEW DIRECTIONS FOR HIGHER EDUCATION • DOI: 10.1002/he

complex and difficult undertaking that fundamentally challenges the dominant operating system of higher education. The shift has implications that are broader than faculty research and scholarship; it has implications for how knowledge is constructed and legitimated, how knowledge is organized in the curriculum, how the curriculum is delivered through instruction, how knowledge is created and shared, and the kind of institutional culture that supports a change in all these educational dimensions. Because of this complexity, shifting institutional identity so that community engagement is both deep and pervasive across the institution is a long and difficult process. It requires long-term commitment, intentionality, and clear understanding of purpose and outcomes.

Evidence from the 2006 applications suggests that campuses intent on encouraging community-engaged scholarship through institutional reward policies should focus their attention in three areas:

- Clearly define the parameters of community-engaged scholarship as a precursor to creating clear and specific criteria for the kinds of evidence faculty need to provide to demonstrate community-engaged scholarship.
- Construct policies that reward community engagement across faculty roles so that research activity will be integrated with teaching and service as seamlessly connected scholarly activity.
- Operationalize the norms of reciprocity in criteria for evaluating community-engaged scholarship, reconceptualizing what is considered as a "publication" and who constitutes a "peer" in the peer review process.

Campuses that incorporate these three dimensions in their institutional reward policies have made a significant transition in transforming the institutional culture to reward community-engaged scholarship. This kind of institutional transformation supports engaged faculty work that contributes not only to the production of new knowledge but to providing a way for American colleges and universities to more effectively fulfill their academic and civic missions.

References

Boyer, E. *Scholarship Reconsidered: Priorities of the Professoriate.* Princeton, N.J.: Carnegie Foundation for the Advancement of Teaching, 1990.

Boyer, E. "The Scholarship of Engagement." *Journal of Public Service and Outreach*, 1996, 1(1), 11–20.

Driscoll, A. "Carnegie's Community-Engagement Classification: Intentions and Insights." *Change: The Magazine of Higher Learning*, 2008, 40(1), 38–41

Driscoll, A., and Lynton, E. (eds.). *Making Outreach Visible: A Workbook on Documenting Professional Service and Outreach.* Washington, D.C.: American Association for Higher Education, 1999.

Eckel, P., Hill, B., and Green, M. *On Change: En Route to Transformation.* Washington, D.C.: American Council on Education, 1998.

Ellison, J., and Eatman, T. K. *Scholarship in Action: Knowledge Creation and Tenure Policy in the Engaged University.* Syracuse, N.Y.: Imagining America, 2008.

Giles, D. E. Jr. "Understanding an Emerging Field of Scholarship: Toward a Research Agenda for Engaged Public Scholarship." *Journal of Higher Education Outreach and Engagement*, 2008, *12*(2), 97–108.

Glassick, C. E., Huber, M. T., and Maeroff, G. *Scholarship Assessed: Evaluation of the Professoriate*. San Francisco: Jossey-Bass, 1997.

Lynton, E. *Making the Case for Professional Service*. Washington, D.C.: American Association for Higher Education, 1995.

O'Meara, K. A. "Service-Learning, Scholarship, and the Reward System." In J. S. Greenberg (ed.), *Service-Learning in Health Education*. Reston Va.: American Association for Health Education, 2000.

O'Meara, K. A. "Uncovering the Values in Faculty Evaluation of Service as Scholarship." *Review of Higher Education*, 2002, *26*(1), 57–80.

O'Meara, K. A. "Reframing Incentives and Rewards for Community Service-Learning and Academic Outreach." *Journal of Higher Education Outreach and Engagement*, 2003, *8*(2), 201–220.

O'Meara, K. A., and Rice, R. E. (eds.). *Faculty Priorities Reconsidered: Encouraging Multiple Forms of Scholarship*. San Francisco: Jossey-Bass, 2005.

Sandmann, L. R. "Conceptualization of the Scholarship of Engagement in Higher Education: A Strategic Review, 1996–2006." *Journal of Higher Education Outreach and Engagement*, 2008, *12*(1), 91–104.

Ward, K. *Faculty Service Roles and the Scholarship of Engagement*. ASHE-ERIC Higher Education Report, 2003, *29*(5).

Ward, K. "Rethinking Faculty Roles and Rewards for the Public Good." In A. J. Kezar and Associates (eds.), *Higher Education and the Public Good: Emerging Voices from a National Movement*. San Francisco: Jossey-Bass, 2005.

Weerts, D. J., and Sandmann, L. R. "Building a Two-Way Street: Challenges and Opportunities for Community Engagement at Research Universities." *Review of Higher Education*, 2008, *32*(1), 73–106.

Weiser, C. J. "The Value System of a University: Rethinking Scholarship." 1996. Retrieved September 19, 2008, from http://www.adec.edu/clemson/papers/weiser.html.

JOHN SALTMARSH *is director of the New England Resource Center for Higher Education in the Graduate College of Education at the University of Massachusetts Boston, where he teaches in the higher education administration doctoral program.*

DWIGHT E. GILES Jr. *is professor of higher education administration and a senior associate at the New England Resource Center for Higher Education in the Graduate College of Education at the University of Massachusetts Boston.*

ELAINE WARD *is a doctoral candidate at the University of Massachusetts Boston's Leadership in Higher Education Program and works at the University's College of Public and Community Service.*

SUZANNE M. BUGLIONE *is a doctoral candidate at the University of Massachusetts Boston's Leadership in Higher Education Program and teaches at Worcester State College in health sciences, education, and sociology. She is principal and lead consultant at CommunityBuild, working with educational, health and human service institutions in the development of capacity, community partnerships, connections, and power.*

NEW DIRECTIONS FOR HIGHER EDUCATION • DOI: 10.1002/he

4

This chapter summarizes institutional best practices in the assessment of service-learning.

Innovative Practices in Service-Learning and Curricular Engagement

Robert G. Bringle, Julie A. Hatcher

As civic and community engagement become more salient within higher education (Colby, Ehrlich, Beaumont, and Stephens, 2003), there is a need to examine critically the core components that allow campuses to realize Ernest Boyer's vision for the new American college that connects its rich resources "to our most pressing social, civic, and ethical problems, to our children, to our schools, to our teachers, to our cities" (1996, pp. 19–20). Boyer's call is aligned with higher education rethinking about how community involvement can change the nature of faculty work, enhance student learning, better fulfill campus mission, and improve the quality of life in communities (Bringle, Games, and Malloy, 1999; Calleson, Jordan, and Seifer, 2005; Colby, Ehrlich, Beaumont, and Stephens, 2003; Edgerton, 1994; Harkavy and Puckett, 1994; O'Meara and Rice, 2005; Percy, Zimpher, and Brukardt, 2006). This civic dimension of higher education is the basis for the Carnegie elective Community Engagement Classification.

Although there are many manifestations of civic and community engagement, curricular engagement in general and service-learning classes in particular are core components as campuses progress beyond traditional models of engagement, such as expert-based approaches to outreach and professional service, that develop broader and deeper impact across the campus and within communities. Broader impact can be demonstrated by evidence of institutional structures to support the development of service-learning courses; the prevalence of service-learning classes across degree programs and schools; the level of participation of students, faculty, and community partners; and the range of community partners, service activities, and social

New Directions for Higher Education, no. 147, Fall 2009 © Wiley Periodicals, Inc.
Published online in Wiley InterScience (www.interscience.wiley.com) • DOI: 10.1002/he.356

issues addressed. Documenting the breadth of impact is accomplished by reporting the number of service-learning classes, the number of students enrolled and hours they contributed to the community, the number of faculty and range of disciplines, and the number of community partners and types of community issues addressed through service-learning. Depth of impact can be demonstrated by the extent to which service-learning is integral to degree programs and majors, faculty work and rewards, student learning outcomes, institutional mission, and long-term reciprocal partnerships with community organizations that address community needs. Documentation of the depth of impact requires more varied forms of evidence, and this is the type of evidence that distinguishes campuses that have received the voluntary classification for community engagement.

As a core component of civic engagement, service-learning is defined as a "course-based, credit bearing educational experience in which students (a) participate in an organized service activity that meets identified community needs, and (b) reflect on the service activity in such a way as to gain further understanding of course content, a broader appreciation of the discipline, and an enhanced sense of personal values and civic responsibility" (Bringle and Hatcher, 1995, p. 112). This definition highlights the academic, curricular nature of service-learning; the importance of community voice in the development, implementation, and assessment of the impact of a service-learning course; the key role that reflection activities play in intentionally connecting the community service activity to reach targeted educational outcomes; and the importance of expanding educational objectives to include civic education. In service-learning, students are not only "serving to learn," which occurs in other forms of curricular engagement and applied learning such as clinical, fieldwork, internship, and practicum, but also "learning to serve," the unique civic dimension of the pedagogy.

Unlike many other forms of practice-based and community-based learning (examples are cooperative education, extension service placements, field education, internships, and practicum), service-learning is integrated into a course and has the intentional goal of developing civic skills and dispositions in students (Battistoni, 2000; Furco, 1996; Westheimer and Kahne, 2003). Unlike cocurricular community service programs (volunteer programs, community outreach, and student service organizations, for example), service-learning is academic work in which the community service activities are used as a "text" that is interpreted, analyzed, and related to the content of a course in ways that permit a formal evaluation of the academic learning outcomes (Furco, 1996; Zlotkowski, 1996).

Although not a new pedagogy (Stanton, Giles, and Cruz, 1999), service-learning has gained prominence in higher education during the past fifteen years with a presence in all institutional types and across all fields of study in American colleges and universities (Campus Compact, 2005; Zlotkowski, 2000). As an academic enterprise, service-learning is a dimension of faculty work that is most broadly defined as civic engagement (see Figure 4.1). Civic

Figure 4.1. Engagement of Faculty Work in and with the Community

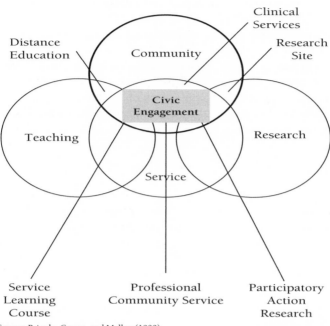

Source: Bringle, Games, and Malloy (1999).

engagement can occur through teaching, research, or service that is done in and with the community and includes a variety of activities (see the Indiana University-Purdue University Indianapolis Web-based Institutional Portfolio at http://www.iport.iupui.edu for sample performance measures and examples of evidence that can be collected to document civic engagement). However, we contend that service-learning provides the most important vehicle of community engagement because

> when service-learning is institutionalized, then it is part of the academic culture of the institution, aligns with the mission, becomes an enduring aspect of the curriculum that is supported by more than a few faculty, improves other forms of pedagogy, leads to other forms of civic scholarship, influences faculty roles and rewards, is part of the experience of most students, and has widespread support, understanding, and involvement of students, faculty, administration, and the community. This leads us to the conclusion that service-learning is, thus, a necessary component of effective civic engagement and, if one cannot measure and evaluate every aspect of civic engagement, then service-learning is the most important critical indicator of a campus's civic engagement [Bringle, Hatcher, Hamilton, and Young, 2001, p. 93].

NEW DIRECTIONS FOR HIGHER EDUCATION • DOI: 10.1002/he

The Carnegie elective Community Engagement Classification endorses the centrality of service-learning in assessing community engagement by devoting one type of classification to curricular engagement and highlighting service-learning courses as the type of evidence that is sought to establish the quantity and quality of curricular engagement. Information is requested about numerous aspects of service-learning on a campus, but these focus primarily on the prevalence and nature of service-learning in the curriculum (individual courses, degree programs, and graduation requirements, for example) and the identification of student learning outcomes and their assessment. We concentrated our analysis of the institutional applications to evidence related to curricular engagement on these two themes.

Prevalence and Nature of Service-Learning Classes

We examined a selection of the applications submitted in the first wave to the Carnegie Foundation for the voluntary classification for community engagement and focused on the information related to curricular engagement. The evidence of curricular engagement in applications provides an important portrait of the status of service-learning in some of the most engaged institutions in American higher education. Capturing the prevalence and nature of service-learning depends on how a campus defines service-learning, how this definition is understood by faculty and staff across departments and schools, and how student enrollment in service-learning classes can be gathered (Zuiches, 2008). Most campuses in the first wave of applications offered their own campus-specific definitions of service-learning (Driscoll, 2008). Some have adopted a broader interpretation and definition of service-learning that includes cocurricular and other activities (Campus Compact, 2003). In all cases, however, service-learning must have an academic component that is integrated with the service activities through structured reflection and must target both academic and civic learning outcomes for students (Bringle, Hatcher, and Clayton, 2006).

Every campus demonstrated in its applications evidence of their capacity to answer questions about the prevalence of service-learning and other forms of community-based instruction, such as community-based research, cooperative education, and internships, even if this information was based on approximations rather than refined data. This is not trivial, for, we would speculate, the mechanism to document service-learning has developed only during the past decade or so. This capacity demonstrates that these institutions have defined service-learning and have the ability to monitor the prevalence of service-learning classes for reasons that predate the Carnegie application (for example, institutional research, accreditation, program evaluation, publicity, and strategic planning) or as a result of the Carnegie application.

The institutional applications also demonstrated that having this information about the prevalence of service-learning classes contributes to other

NEW DIRECTIONS FOR HIGHER EDUCATION • DOI: 10.1002/he

purposes of the institution, including accreditation, program review, and publicity about community engagement to external audiences (community leaders, community partners, and prospective students, for example), information for funding allocations and resources (the board of trustees, granting agencies, and legislators, among others), and internal purposes (including annual reports, benchmarking, faculty roles and rewards, recognition, and strategic planning). Most important, perhaps, this level of documentation increases the capacity for institutional assessment of student learning outcomes and community impact of service-learning.

Quantifying the prevalence of service-learning and community-based instruction presents a perplexing challenge. First, numbers of courses matter for some important purposes, but they are very limited in their implications for assessing the quality of curricular engagement and the quality of learning derived from curricular engagement. Concerning number of courses, the ideal aspiration would be that service-learning has a presence that is evenly distributed across academic units rather than clustered in a few and across various levels of the curriculum (first year, major, capstone, and graduate). Simply reporting the number of service-learning classes provides little information about the vertical distribution of those courses (within the curriculum of a major or degree program) or the horizontal distribution (across academic units, across community issues). We saw few examples of campuses organizing their data in this manner. In addition, only limited information was shared about how service-learning courses are aligned with the mission of the campus, and even less evidence as to how service-learning is responsive to community priorities or pressing social issues (Boyer, 1996). Revisions and additional questions in the Carnegie classification process now probe for this type of information. Such a mapping of vertical and horizontal density and the evenness of distribution was largely lacking in the first wave of documentation, but having this information will offer insight into the degree of institutional support of service-learning classes beyond merely counting the number of courses, students, faculty, and community partners.

Some campuses provided evidence in their applications on the development of multicourse curricula that focus on the learning outcomes most clearly aligned with civic engagement: community-based leadership, public service, study of the nonprofit sector, and community service studies. Many of these programs incorporate service-learning as the sole or dominant pedagogy of the curriculum. These new certificates, majors, and degree programs, coupled with programs and initiatives that reexamine and enhance the civic engagement of existing majors and departments, represent significant curricular innovations beyond the revision of isolated service-learning courses. The advantage of these curricular innovations is that they are intentional, coherent, and sequenced curricular developments that represent support from a number of instructors and faculty within and across

NEW DIRECTIONS FOR HIGHER EDUCATION • DOI: 10.1002/he

departments or programs. This movement toward an "engaged department" strategy represents an important development for resource allocation (Battistoni and others, 2003; Kecskes, 2004) and has implications for faculty development programs designed to support the integration of service-learning across the curriculum.

In addition, the documentation in the first wave of applications provides many examples for how the development of service-learning is linked to other curricular initiatives and cocurricular programs on campus. These include first-year success seminars, large-enrollment first-year courses, thematic learning communities, general education requirements, capstone courses, diversity initiatives, orientation programs, undergraduate research programs, international study abroad, and service-based scholarship programs. All of these are significant advances in curricular innovation beyond the integration of service-learning into an isolated course. These institutional strategies broaden the discussion and participation of faculty and staff and demonstrate the support of executive leadership who value service-learning as having a significant role in many areas of campus work. Whether it starts with mission, strategic planning, institutional problem solving (academic success and retention are two examples), individual faculty members, or helping academic units do their work better, service-learning is now recognized as an active learning strategy to achieve a wide range of campus goals.

Learning Outcomes and Assessment in Service-Learning

One type of quality control evident in documentation is how campuses support the development and implementation of service-learning courses. Most campuses reported strategies in their applications to support faculty development: faculty fellows programs, internal course development grants, and training sessions and workshops are examples. In addition, some campuses provided guidelines for service-learning courses and document a process to review course syllabi in order to designate a course as a service-learning course. Whether through a faculty advisory committee or at the campus level, such as a program review committee or curriculum review, this type of course review increases the capacity to formally designate service-learning courses in course bulletins or on student transcripts. These institutional strategies are based on the assumption that if a course is well designed and meets the designated criteria of a service-learning course, the course is more likely to produce desired outcomes for students and community partners on implementation.

The evidence offered to evaluate the degree to which service-learning courses and other community-based courses meet intended learning outcomes mirrors general practice in higher education for gathering these types of evidence. Assessment is heavily dependent, first and foremost, on self-report instruments that students complete, usually at the end of the semester.

This assessment may be general student satisfaction surveys or surveys tailored to service-learning. There were examples in the applications of surveys that were specifically developed within a course, common to a set of courses, or centrally distributed to all service-learning courses on a campus. Furthermore, the evidence offered about the use of this information was typically speculative, and the process of using the feedback to redesign and improve a course was not implemented in a systematic or programmatic manner. In addition, our analysis and that of Driscoll (2008) found little evidence of community impact through service-learning courses, a void that is consistent with the lack of community input and voice across all of the applications submitted to Carnegie in the first wave.

In addition to a common end-of-semester survey that permits the aggregation of data across the curriculum, some campuses reported using other sources of evidence to monitor student learning outcomes. In general, there is some, but at this point quite limited, evidence of how assessment of curricular engagement is coordinated with, linked to, or supported by other forms of institutional assessment and research. Some campuses integrate questions about service-learning involvement in either entering student or graduating student surveys. The National Survey of Student Engagement (NSSE) is one of many instruments that can be used to document institutional accountability in civic engagement. NSSE was cited and used as an institutional assessment strategy by some campuses in the first wave of documentation. This survey has the advantage that the results permit comparisons with peer institutions, and it becomes possible to link results of NSSE to other institutional data, such as surveys from service-learning courses and student transcripts. However, NSEE and other similar surveys, including the Beginning College Survey of Student Engagement and Community College Survey of Student Engagement, are limited in that they capture the level of activities as self-reported by students, focus on engagement as general student involvement in campus and classroom activities rather than civic engagement, and are not designed to explore directly the impact of these activities on student learning outcomes (see http://www.csl.iupui.edu for a sample listing of accountability tools for civic engagement and other surveys used in higher education).

Documentation of curricular engagement will be improved when methods are employed for collecting information on student learning that is evaluated by an independent source rather than students' self-reports. Very few studies currently provide this documentation, although the Carnegie documents do establish that research and scholarship are being conducted on service-learning by faculty and staff that is contributing to a growing body of knowledge (see the National Service-learning Clearinghouse at www.servicelearning.org for resources on conducting research). Almost nonexistent in the applications was the capacity to answer questions about learning at the level of the program (within a major or across the general education curriculum; Katz-Jameson, Clayton, and Bringle, 2008) or institution.

Attempts to evaluate student development and learning over time for a cohort of students are only beginning to develop (Terkla, O'Leary, Wilson, and Diaz, 2007; Wilson, Diaz, O'Leary, and Terkla, 2007), and evidence about the effects of curricular engagement in the postgraduation behaviors and attitudes of students is extremely limited (Astin, Sax, and Avolos, 1999; Vogelgesang and Astin, 2000).

Service-learning provides an excellent opportunity for developing procedures to assess the civic outcomes of service-learning at the course, department, and institutional levels. As Cunningham (2006) notes,

> One of [the] goals is the broad-based education of students to be effective engaged citizens in our democratic society, and to be good citizens in our increasingly international world. Civic learning outcomes from higher education are difficult to document, but they are one of the most important social and civic contributions our colleges and universities provide to our society [p. 4].

Again, most evidence provided in the applications on civic learning outcomes consisted of self-report measures of attitudes and beliefs at the course level; there was little evidence at the program or institutional level and no evidence of longitudinal research in materials submitted to Carnegie. Future work on measuring civic outcomes of curricular engagement should specify the learning outcomes germane to the civic domain (Battistoni, 2001; Kirlin, 2003) and identify the knowledge, skills, and dispositions of civic-minded graduates (Bringle and Steinberg, forthcoming; Hatcher and Steinberg, 2007). This work is also being addressed by two working groups convened by the American Association of Colleges and Universities and the American Association of State Colleges and Universities. The goal of these groups is to develop rubrics for civic learning outcomes. Once they are developed, campuses can use or modify these rubrics to evaluate student products such as electronic portfolios and written narratives as authentic evidence that is collected through a structured reflection process, with these products evaluated in a systematic way (see Ash, Clayton, and Atkinson, 2005) to evaluate student learning.

Conclusion

The documentation that campuses provided in the first wave of the Carnegie elective Community Engagement Classification demonstrates that service-learning is a valued pedagogy for engaged campuses. Service-learning is viewed as central to community engagement not only because it is a core component of the Carnegie elective classification but also because many institutions now have the infrastructure to support the development of service-learning classes. The prevalence of service-learning is readily documented, an important step toward the institutionalization of service-learning in higher education (Bringle and Hatcher, 1995).

NEW DIRECTIONS FOR HIGHER EDUCATION • DOI: 10.1002/he

There is now a need to go beyond mere counting to develop strategies to assess the quality of service-learning experiences for students, faculty, institutions, and communities. There is also a need to move from course assessment to institutional assessment and research at the program and institutional levels. In addition, institutions need to move from student self-report measures to more authentic forms of evidence, such as student products or responses to structured narrative reflection prompts, that capture student learning. These developments will position curricular engagement to contribute to and improve how the academy thinks about learning outcomes, curricular development, assessment, and community impact.

References

Ash, A. L., Clayton, P. H., and Atkinson, M. P. "Integrating Reflection and Assessment to Capture and Improve Student Learning." *Michigan Journal of Community Service-Learning*, 2005, *11*(2), 49–60.

Astin, A. W., Sax, L. J., and Avolos, J. "Long Term Effects of Volunteerism During the Undergraduate Years." *Review of Higher Education*, 1999, 22(2), 187–202.

Battistoni, R. M. "Service-Learning and Civic Education." In S. Mann and J. Patrick (eds.), *Education for Civic Engagement in Democracy: Service-Learning and Other Promising Practices*. Bloomington, Ind.: ERIC Clearinghouse for Social Studies/Social Science Education, 2000. (ED 447 065)

Battistoni, R. M. *Civic Engagement Across the Curriculum: A Resource Book for Service-Learning Faculty in All Disciplines*. Providence, R.I.: Campus Compact, 2001.

Battistoni, R. M., and others. *The Engaged Department Toolkit*. Providence, R.I.: Campus Compact, 2003.

Boyer, E. L. "The Scholarship of Engagement." *Journal of Public Service and Outreach*, 1996, *1*(1), 11–20.

Bringle, R. G., Games, R., and Malloy, E. A. "Colleges and Universities as Citizens: Issues and Perspectives." In R. G. Bringle, R. Games, and E. A. Malloy (eds.), *Colleges and Universities as Citizens*. Needham Heights, Mass.: Allyn & Bacon, 1999.

Bringle, R. G., and Hatcher, J. A. "A Service-Learning Curriculum for Faculty." *Michigan Journal of Community Service-learning*, 1995, 2, 112–122.

Bringle, R. G., Hatcher, J. A., and Clayton, P. H. "The Scholarship of Civic Engagement: Defining, Documenting, and Evaluating Faculty Work." *To Improve the Academy*, 2006, *25*, 257–279.

Bringle, R. G., Hatcher, J. A., Hamilton, S., and Young, P. "Planning and Assessing Campus/Community Engagement." *Metropolitan Universities*, 2001, *12*(3), 89–99.

Bringle, R. G., and Steinberg, K. "Educating for Informed Community Involvement." *American Journal of Community Psychology*, forthcoming.

Calleson, D. C., Jordan, C., and Seifer, S. D. "Community-Engaged Scholarship: Is Faculty Work in Communities a True Academic Enterprise?" *Academic Medicine*, 2005, *80*(4), 317–321.

Campus Compact. *Introduction to Service-Learning Toolkit: Readings and Resources for Faculty, Second Edition*. Providence, R.I.: Brown University, 2003.

Campus Compact. *Season of Service*. Providence, R.I.: Campus Compact, 2005.

Colby, A., Ehrlich, T., Beaumont, E., and Stephens, J. *Educating Citizens: Preparing America's Undergraduates for Lives of Moral and Civic Responsibility*. San Francisco: Jossey-Bass, 2003.

Cunningham, A. "The Broader Societal Benefits of Higher Education." 2006. Retrieved July 8, 2008, from http://www.solutionsforourfuture.org/site/DocServer/07.Social-Benefits.pdf?docID=102.

Driscoll, A. "Carnegie's Community-Engagement Classification: Intentions and Insights." *Change: The Magazine of Higher Learning, 2008, 40*(1), pp. 38–41.

Edgerton, R. "The Engaged Campus: Organizing to Serve Society's Needs." *AAHE Bulletin,* 1994, *47,* 2–3.

Furco, A. "Service-Learning: A Balanced Approach to Experiential Education." In Corporation for National Service (ed.), *Expanding Boundaries: Serving and Learning.* Columbia, Md.: Cooperative Education Association, 1996.

Harkavy, I., and Puckett, J. L. "Lessons from Hull House for the Contemporary Urban University." *Social Science Review,* 1994, *68,* 299–321.

Hatcher, J. A., and Steinberg, K. S. "Measuring the Concepts Civic-Minded Graduate and Civic-Minded Professional." Workshop presented at the Seventh Annual International Research Conference on Service-Learning and Community Engagement, Oct. 2007, Tampa, Fla.

Katz-Jameson, J., Clayton, P. H., and Bringle, R. G. "Investigating Student Learning Within and Across Linked Service-Learning Courses." In M. A. Bowdon, S. H. Billig, and B. A. Holland (eds.), *Scholarship for Sustaining Service-learning and Civic Engagement.* Charlotte, N.C.: Information Age, 2008.

Kecskes, K. (ed.). *Engaging Departments: Moving Faculty Culture from Private to Public, Individual to Collective Focus for the Common Good.* San Francisco: Anker/Jossey-Bass, 2004.

Kirlin, M. "The Role of Civic Skills in Fostering Civic Engagement." Baltimore, Md.: University of Maryland, Center for Information and Research on Civic Learning and Engagement, 2003.

O'Meara, K., and Rice, R. E. (eds.). *Faculty Priorities Reconsidered: Rewarding Multiple Forms of Scholarship.* San Francisco: Jossey-Bass, 2005.

Percy, S. L., Zimpher, N. L., and Brukardt, M. J. *Creating a New Kind of University: Institutionalizing Community-University Engagement.* San Francisco: Anker/Jossey-Bass, 2006.

Stanton, T. K., Giles, D. E., Jr., and Cruz, N. I. *Service-Learning: A Movement's Pioneers Reflect on Its Origins, Practice, and Future.* San Francisco: Jossey-Bass, 1999.

Terkla, D. G., O'Leary, L. S., Wilson, N. E., and Diaz, A. "Civic Engagement: Linking Activities to Attitudes." *Assessment Update: Progress, Trends, and Practices in Higher Education,* 2007, *19*(3), 1–2, 14–16.

Vogelgesang, L. J., and Astin, A. W. "Comparing the Effects of Community Service and Service-Learning." *Michigan Journal of Community Service-learning,* 2000, *7,* 25–34.

Westheimer, J., and Kahne, J. "What Kind of Citizen? Political Choices and Educational Goals." *Campus Compact Reader,* Winter 2003, pp. 1–13.

Wilson, N. E., Diaz, A., O'Leary, L. S., and Terkla, D. G. "Civic Engagement: A Study of Changes in College." *Academic Exchange Quarterly,* 2007, *11*(2), 141–146.

Zlotkowski, E. "Linking Service-Learning and the Academy: A New Voice at the Table?" *Change: The Magazine of Higher Learning,* 1996, *28*(1), 20–27.

Zlotkowski, E. "Service-Learning in the Disciplines. Strategic Directions for Service-Learning Research." [Special issue]. *Michigan Journal of Community Service-learning,* Fall 2000, pp. 61–67.

Zuiches, J. J. "Attaining Carnegie's Community-Engagement Classification." *Change: The Magazine of Higher Learning, 2008, 40*(1) 42–45.

ROBERT G. BRINGLE *is the executive director of the Center for Service and Learning at Indiana University–Purdue University Indianapolis and a Chancellor's Professor of Psychology and Philanthropic Studies.*

JULIE A. HATCHER *is the associate director of the Center for Service and Learning at Indiana University–Purdue University Indianapolis and an adjunct instructor for philanthropic studies.*

5

A range of instruments and strategies has been employed to benchmark and measure the institutionalization of community engagement.

Issues in Benchmarking and Assessing Institutional Engagement

Andrew Furco, William Miller

Colleges and universities with institutionalized community engagement have (1) a philosophy and mission that emphasizes engagement; (2) genuine faculty involvement and support for engaged research or teaching, or both; (3) a broad range of opportunities for students to access and involve themselves in high-quality engagement experiences; (4) an institutional infrastructure that supports engagement practice; and (5) mutually beneficial, sustained partnerships with community partners (Holland, 2001). These five foundational components work synergistically to build and sustain an institutional culture in which community-engaged research, teaching, and public service are valued to the extent that they become fully infused within the academic fabric of a higher education institution.

While attention to each of these foundational components is essential for fully institutionalizing community engagement, the emphasis placed on each component varies among institutions, based on each one's particular engagement goals and purposes. For example, at some institutions, community engagement is used to improve teaching efficacy or conduct more research in the public interest. At others, it is used to advance faith-based missions, improve town-gown relations, address local emergencies and crises, or develop an ethic of volunteerism and service among students.

We thank Sharon Fross, vice president for academic affairs at the Art Institute of Pittsburgh, and Lisa Burton and Laurel Hirt at the University of Minnesota for their assistance with this chapter.

NEW DIRECTIONS FOR HIGHER EDUCATION, no. 147, Fall 2009 © Wiley Periodicals, Inc.
Published online in Wiley InterScience (www.interscience.wiley.com) • DOI: 10.1002/he.357

47

Consequently, each foundational component assumes particular character-istics depending on an institution's engagement priorities.

To help ensure that the components take shape in ways that best facil-itate the advancement of community engagement, the employment of an assessment process that can measure and benchmark each component's development is essential. An assessment process provides the means to con-duct a status check of the campus's overall current level of community engagement institutionalization by offering a structure and framework for collecting and reviewing information so that informed decisions can be made about an institution's engagement strengths and weaknesses.

The process of assessing and benchmarking community engagement can take many forms. To date, more than two dozen assessment tools for measuring community engagement institutionalization have been pub-lished. These tools vary substantially in purpose, level of complexity, scope, process, structure, and focus. While some instruments are designed to serve as simple and quick on-the-spot assessments (in the form of checklists, for example), other instruments, such as the Carnegie community engagement framework, are much more multifaceted, multilayered assessments that require extensive data gathering and systematic analyses applied over an extended period of time. The Carnegie community engagement framework itself, along with other assessment tools, is examined in this chapter, as well as insights that the 2006 Carnegie community engagement applications pro-vide into the processes and role of assessment in their engagement efforts.

Approaches to Assessing Community Engagement Institutionalization

Burack and Saltmarsh (2006) suggest that because of diverse interests and motivations for assessing the nature and status of campus community engagement, inevitably there will be a multiplicity of approaches to bench-marking the institutionalization of community engagement. In their recent review of engagement institutionalization, they highlight eleven instruments that have been used as self-assessment tools to measure campus community engagement institutionalization. All eleven tools incorporate the five foun-dational components to some degree, yet they approach the assessment process quite differently. Self-assessments are instruments intended to be used by campus members and their partners to conduct internally focused assessments of their institution's community-engaged work. However, many of these tools are increasingly being used for externally driven assessments of community engagement.

About one-third of the community engagement assessment instruments are checklists, which offer a quick and relatively easy way to assess an insti-tution's community engagement institutionalization level. Typically check-lists are composed of a set of components or principles deemed essential for advancing and institutionalizing community engagement. The premise is that the greater the number of components or principles present at the institution, the more institutionalized community engagement is considered to be. The Dimensions of Engagement list, developed as part of the Kellogg Forum on Higher Education for the Public Good (London, 2002), is an example of a checklist. Although checklists are quick and relatively easy to use, they lack rich descriptions, are highly subject to assessor interpretation, are inappropriate for measuring progress over time, and provide no information on extent or degree of institutionalization.

A small set of instruments can be described as indicators. Like checklists, indicators are based on a set of principles that can be organized as measurable components or aspects of specific themes, categories, or constructs. These instruments tend to offer a more robust picture of areas of specific engagement strengths and weaknesses than are provided by checklists. The presence of several related indicators would provide evidence that institutionalization is high for a particular engagement theme or construct; the absence of those same indicators suggests that engagement institutionalization is low for that construct. One challenge with indicator-type assessments is that they sometimes underestimate institutions' levels of engagement. This is because the scoring process is based on an indicator being present or not present. Therefore, a campus for which the indicators are only partially evident in a category will be scored the same as a campus with no indicators in that category. Campus Compact's *Indicators of Engagement* (Hollander, Saltmarsh, and Zlotkowski, 2001) is one widely used approach to assessing the institutionalization of engagement that employs indicators.

The benchmark approach is distinguished from the checklist and indicators approaches in that it calls for more formalized assessment procedures, typically requires presentation of more empirical data, and introduces the notion of performance expectations that can be established through internal or external comparisons. Because the presentation of evidence that demonstrates institutional commitment to engagement is required, this approach tends to produce more precise and accurate conclusions about a campus level of community engagement institutionalization than is found in other assessment approaches. One example of the benchmark approach to community engagement assessment is the Committee on Institutional Collaboration's *Benchmarks on Engagement* (Civic Engagement Benchmarking Task Force, 2005). This type of assessment, which provides evidence for review, is often used by accreditation boards or external review panels.

Another category of instruments is rubrics. Rubrics are distinguished from the previous approaches in that they are inherently two-dimensional, offering more than one point of reference for assessing community engagement institutionalization. Items or statements about community engagement are presented through characterizations of what they might look like at lower and higher levels of institutionalization, forming a table that presents levels of institutionalization for a group of items or statements. Although several assessment rubrics focus on specific issues and aspects of the engagement enterprise (for example, service-learning, community partnerships, faculty development, institutional commitment, and institutional capacity for engagement), only a small number of them focus on broader, more comprehensive issues of community engagement. The depth gained by the greater detail generally contained in rubrics is often lost in breadth and comprehensiveness. One of the more comprehensive engagement assessment rubrics is the *Building Capacity for Community Engagement: Institutional Self-Assessment* (Gelmon, Seifer, Kauper-Brown, and Mikkelsen, 2005), an expanded version of the more focused *Self-Assessment Rubric for Institutionalizing Service-Learning in Higher Education* (Furco, 1998). Rubrics are flexible and allow the calculation of a numerical institutionalization score as well as productions of a qualitative assessment. They lend themselves well to measuring changes in engagement institutionalization over time and are especially useful for conducting multi-institutional comparisons of community engagement institutionalization; however, they require an investment of time and energy to complete, as well as assessor familiarity with the instrument.

Matrices are similar to rubrics in that they present a two-dimensional instrument with a set of engagement factors or components as one dimension and descriptive stages for determining the level of institutionalization (low to high) for each factor. They are distinct from rubrics in that the factors are not constructed with consistent descriptions across the different stages or levels of institutionalization. The descriptions found at the different levels of each factor shift in their focus, and each addresses a different set of issues and circumstances. Matrices are especially useful for action planning in that they identify which component will require attention at particular stages of institutionalization. In addition, because they focus on broad dimensions of institutionalization rather than the levels of development for individual engagement components, matrices are more streamlined than rubrics and are useful for more comprehensive engagement assessment. One of the more widely used engagement assessment matrices is the Levels of Commitment to Engagement matrix (Holland, 1997).

Finally, several engagement assessment tools have been designed as systems that encompass a battery of instruments, procedures, and approaches to provide a more comprehensive assessment, seeking to capture both the depth and breadth of an institution's engagement. Some systems focus exclusively on assessing the institutionalization of engagement (one is the Carnegie classification framework), while other systems focus on specific aspects of the engagement enterprise *Shumer's Self-Assessment Survey for Service-Learning* (Shumer and others, 2000), Indiana University-Purdue University Indianapolis's *Comprehensive Assessment of the Scholarship of Engagement* (Bringle and Hatcher, 1999), and Furco's *Evaluation System for Experiential Education* (Furco, 1997). Usually the systems approach calls for data based on historic documents, interviews of key stakeholders, group discussions on the purpose of engagement, and various questionnaires and surveys. Although these more comprehensive assessment systems provide an evidence-based picture of the breadth, depth, and scope of an institution's engagement efforts, they require substantial time and effort as well as skilled assessors.

Assessment Considerations from Carnegie Classified Institutions

The systems approach of the Carnegie community engagement process offers both a universal framework for assessing community engagement that can be applied across institutions and a flexibility to be adapted to different kinds of institutions in ways that capture their individual contexts. For this latter reason, it is not surprising that a variety of assessment approaches were discussed in the first wave of community engagement applications. Although few campuses mentioned the specific tools reviewed earlier in this chapter, many institutions had developed their own indicators, databases, or other tracking mechanisms. Institutions used such mechanisms to address internal needs, external requirements, or both. Regardless of the approach used to assess the institutionalization level of a campus's community engagement effort, several issues should be considered in order to ensure that the assessment process is successful. Examples from the Carnegie community engagement applications are included and exemplify the importance of these considerations.

Defining Terms. Effective assessment requires a shared understanding of concepts and terminology. In its community engagement application to the Carnegie Foundation, North Carolina State University defines *community engagement* as "a responsive relationship bringing the University into mutually-beneficial partnerships with place-based or area-of-interest based communities." It emphasizes a broad conception of community in the sense of "interest, practice, and purpose" as opposed to "community" that is defined by geographical boundaries. The process of definition likely takes on added significance when framed within an institution's strategic planning process or vision. For example, University of Alaska Anchorage developed an academic plan for 2005–2009 that identified community engagement as one of four core priorities. This priority is defined as "being fully engaged in the economic, cultural, and civic life of communities the institution serves" and also "serving as a setting for public discourse, a venue for artistic expressions and a partner in community endeavors." In both cases, definitions influence both processes and measures in their respective assessment strategies.

Timing. Careful consideration should be given as to when the institutional assessment is conducted. The 2006 applications of Carnegie community-engaged institutions showed that assessment practices were often decentralized and occurred at the program level as opposed to a more coordinated or systematic approach at the institutional level. Virginia Tech and Michigan State provide notable exceptions to this finding, with assessment for community engagement more fully integrated into routine systems for faculty reporting and institutional strategic planning. Studies of community engagement institutionalization reveal that it takes about fifteen years of concentrated effort for community engagement to be fully institutionalized into a college or university (Furco, 2002; Percy, Zimpher, and Brukardt, 2006). If this is true, then conducting an assessment of community engagement too early in the institutionalization process may present disappointing results. Nevertheless, regular assessment allows an institution to develop a record of progress.

Purpose. As evidenced in the 2006 Carnegie community engagement applications, community engagement may be assessed as part of continuous improvement, action planning, accreditation, impact assessment, and grant reporting. The purposes of assessment influence which approaches will be most viable, what kinds of data will need to be collected, and which data analysis procedures will be most appropriate. The purposes also influence the regularity of assessment, that is, whether it is episodic or a routine part of institutional data collection. Purpose also has an impact on the scale and scope of the assessment, for example, the need to focus on the broad range of community engagement efforts or on specific issues (faculty, community partnerships, service-learning, and so forth).

Purpose may also influence whether data are collected internally or by an external entity. Tufts University's 2006 Carnegie application describes a longitudinal study on students' civic and political activities and attitudes. Such longitudinal studies can often serve multiple purposes and can serve to make the assessment of community engagement a more routine and integral part of university life. Specific purposes, such as documenting changes in undergraduate learning experiences, should necessarily be reflected in the design of the assessment approach. Considering these and related issues about the purposes and audience of the assessment will help determine which assessment approaches and instruments will be most appropriate.

Assessors. Generally the 2006 Carnegie community-engaged institutions employed existing internal capacities in the assessment of community engagement efforts. Notable exceptions were Widener University, Arizona State, and the University of Wisconsin-Parkside, which included the use of external review teams. Whether assessors are conducting an internally focused self-assessment or an external assessment, they view the evidence and data before them to make a justifiable judgment on the result. Therefore, those who facilitate the assessment must be skillful and knowledgeable in several areas. They must understand community engagement and how it is being operationalized at the institution where the assessment is taking place. They must understand the nature of communities where the institution is located and the history of the institution's relationship with the community. They need to have access to the people and archives that can provide the necessary data needed to complete the assessment. If the

NEW DIRECTIONS FOR HIGHER EDUCATION • DOI: 10.1002/he

assessment is conducted internally as a self-assessment, inviting external assessors to offer their feedback and review can help reduce potential biases.

Adapting Tools. Many of the available assessment tools are meant to be adapted to meet the individual needs of the institution; not all components of an assessment tool are equally important in various contexts and at various times. In addition, terminology used in the instruments may be different from what is used at the institution and require adaptation. For example, over the years, several versions of Furco's self-assessment rubric for institutionalizing service-learning in higher education (1998) have become available as assessment teams have modified the tool to adapt it to their individual institutional needs. In some versions, the term *service-learning* has been replaced by the particular engagement terms used at the institution, for example, *academic service-learning, community-based learning,* or *community internships.* Other modifications of the rubric include a reconfiguration of the instrument's original three-level continuum (critical mass building, quality building, and sustained institutionalization) into a nine-level continuum that can capture more incremental institutionalization progress within a shorter time period and the addition of new components (such as assessing the strength of service-learning partnerships in a particular neighbor) that address unique issues at the institutions. Those who adapt tools to meet institutional goals should take care not to change the intent of what is being asked or required. In addition, portions of the assessment may be eliminated if deemed irrelevant to the context of the institution or the assessment; they should not be eliminated solely because they are too complicated to address or that they might reveal some negative aspects of the institution's engagement effort.

Conclusion

The assessment process itself is an important part of the institutionalization of community engagement. The 2006 Carnegie classification process and applications have solidified the importance of assessment and illuminated areas for improvement and future consideration. Regardless of the approach used to conduct an assessment of community engagement, assessment must be coupled with action planning, whereby the information garnered from the assessment is used strategically to make decisions that can advance community engagement at the institution. As was evidenced at many of the institutions where the Carnegie assessment was applied, the process instigated the formalization of institutional goals and definitions for community engagement and resulted in the development of institutional strategic plans for community engagement.

Clear intentions about the purposes and uses for the assessment to be conducted will help ensure that the most appropriate approach to assessment is used. In most cases, the process of conducting the assessment will provide many useful data and information about the status of community engagement, often more than the final results from the assessment instrument will reveal. Periodic and ongoing assessment at the institutional level will provide important information about how community engagement is evolving and which aspects of it are gaining strength and which are weakening. When done thoughtfully, systematically, and periodically, assessment can hold the key to securing a promising and positive trajectory for advancing the institutionalization of community engagement in higher education.

References

Bringle, R., and Hatcher, J. A. *Comprehensive Assessment of the Scholarship of Engagement (CASE)*. Indianapolis: Indiana University-Purdue University, Indianapolis, 1999.

Burack, C., and Saltmarsh, J. *Assessing the Institutionalization of Civic Engagement*. Boston: University of Massachusetts Boston, 2006.

Civic Engagement Benchmarking Task Force. *Resource Guide and Recommendations for Defining and Benchmarking Engagement*. CIC Committee on Engagement in collaboration with National Association of State Universities and Land Grant Colleges: Council on Extension, Continuing Education, and Public Service Benchmarking Task Force. 2005. Retrieved November 29, 2008, from http://www.cic.uiuc.edu/groups/CommitteeOnEngagement/index.shtml.

Furco, A. *Evaluation System for Experiential Education*. Berkeley: Service-Learning Research and Development Center, University of California at Berkeley, 1997.

Furco, A. *Self-Assessment Rubric for the Institutionalization of Service-Learning in Higher Education*. Berkeley: Service-Learning Research and Development Center, University of California at Berkeley, 1998.

Furco, A. "Institutionalizing Service-Learning in Higher Education." *Journal of Public Affairs*, 2002, 6, 39–67.

Gelmon, S. B., Seifer, S. D., Kauper-Brown, J., and Mikkelsen, M. *Building Capacity for Community Engagement: Institutional Self-Assessment*. Seattle, Wash.: Community-Campus Partnerships for Health, 2005.

Holland, B. "Analyzing Institutional Commitment to Engagement: A Model of Key Organizational Factors." *Michigan Journal of Community Service Learning*, 1997, 4, 30–41.

Holland, B. A. "A Comprehensive Model for Assessing Service-Learning and Community-University Partnerships." *New Directions for Higher Education*, 2001, 114, 51–60.

Hollander, E. L., Saltmarsh, J., and Zlotkowski, E. "Indicators of Engagement." In L. A. Simon, M. Kenny, K. Brabeck, & R. M. Lerner (eds.), *Learning to Serve: Promoting Civil Society Through Service-Learning*. Norwell, Mass.: Kluwer, 2001.

London, S. *Practical Strategies for Institutional Civic Engagement and Institutional Leadership That Reflect and Shape the Covenant Between Higher Education and Society*. Monticello, Minn.: Kellogg Forum on Higher Education for the Public Good, 2002.

Percy, S. L., Zimpher, N. L., and Brukardt, M. J. (eds.). *Creating a New Kind of University: Institutionalizing Community-University Engagement*. San Francisco: Anker/Jossey-Bass, 2006.

Shumer, R., and others. *Shumer's Self-Assessment for Service-Learning*. St. Paul, Minn.: Center for Experiential and Service-Learning, 2000.

Andrew Furco is associate professor of educational policy and administration at the University of Minnesota, where he also serves as associate vice president for public engagement and director of the International Center for Research on Community Engagement.

William Miller is director of extension planning and evaluation at the University of Massachusetts Amherst.

6

This chapter describes various community-campus partnerships and offers practical recommendations for forming and evaluating reciprocal relationships.

Understanding and Enhancing the Opportunities of Community-Campus Partnerships

Carole Beere

Despite the fact that universities and their various communities have much to offer and much to gain from partnering, the number of submissions for the Carnegie elective Community Engagement Classification suggests that partnerships are not ubiquitous in higher education. This is not surprising. Creating a productive, healthy, and sustainable partnership is hard work and time-consuming. Universities and communities are often unaware of the potential of partnerships or lack the knowledge or commitment necessary for their development. Partnerships are less efficient than working alone. But productive partnerships exemplify the notion that the whole is greater than the sum of the parts. That is, campus and community can accomplish more together than either could do alone.

This chapter defines partnership, provides an overview of the partnership-related data reported to Carnegie, and offers recommendations for universities, their partners in the community, and the Carnegie Foundation for the Advancement of Teaching to strengthen and advance such partnerships for the future.

Defining *Partnership*

Definitions of *partnership* vary, but almost all include three essential elements: (1) a relationship, characterized by mutuality, (2) involving two or more individuals, groups, or organizations, that share (3) a commitment to

NEW DIRECTIONS FOR HIGHER EDUCATION, no. 147, Fall 2009 © Wiley Periodicals, Inc.
Published online in Wiley InterScience (www.interscience.wiley.com) • DOI: 10.1002/he.358

an agreed-on goal or purpose. Partnerships can be formal or informal, large or small, short term or long lasting, focused on a single goal or serving multiple purposes. Tyler and Haberman (2002) suggest that partnerships "can be grouped along the following continuum: (1) committed, (2) supportive, (3) indifferent, (4) protective, and (5) exploitive" (p. 89). Large, complex partnerships might have elements of all of these, but clearly the first two types are desirable and are much more likely to lead to achieving agreed-on goals than are the last three, which are counterproductive.

The Carnegie Foundation states that "partnership focuses on collaborative interactions with community and related scholarship for the mutually beneficial exchange, exploration, and application of knowledge, information, and resources (research, capacity building, economic development, etc.)" (Carnegie, 2008). The 2006 applications provide a means for examining trends and best practices around the formation and success of partnerships between higher education institutions and communities.

Partnership in the Carnegie Framework

Carnegie's 2006 application for the elective Community Engagement Classification requested descriptions of "representative partnerships (both institutional and departmental) that were in place during the most recent academic year (maximum 20 partnerships)." What constituted a "representative partnership" was left to the discretion of each campus completing the application. It is not clear how the limit of twenty partnerships had an impact on the conclusions drawn here, but it is reasonable to assume that campuses listed what they considered to be their most successful partnerships.

For each of the listed partnerships, campuses were asked to provide partnership name, community partners, institutional partners, purpose, length of partnership, number of faculty, number of students, grant funding, institutional impact, and community impact. I discuss all but the last two of these, because there was limited to no variability in responses. In almost all cases, institutions talked about the positive impact of the partnerships, although many instances were offered that noted the results of the partnership could not yet be identified.

Understanding and comparing some data in the applications was difficult. This was particularly true for "number of faculty" (many listed staff as well as faculty, and some listed the number involved in a single year, while others listed the number involved during the life of the partnership); "number of students" (some reported only students who were working on the partnership, while others included students who were the recipients of partnership services; some listed those participating in a single year while others listed those participating throughout the life of the partnership); and "grant funding" (some listed only externally funded grants, some listed internally funded grants, and in some cases, the source of the grant was unclear).

After describing the partnerships, applicants were asked to respond to three yes-no questions and describe examples when checking yes:

1. "Does the institution or do the departments work to promote the mutuality and reciprocity of the partnerships?" This is a critical question, as mutuality is a defining characteristic of a true partnership.
2. "Are there mechanisms to systematically provide feedback and assessment to community partners?" Systematic feedback and assessment are part of the evaluation process, which is important to strengthening and sustaining a partnership.
3. "Are there examples of faculty scholarship associated with their outreach and partnership activities (technical reports, curriculum, research reports, policy developments, journal publications, etc.)?" Evidence of faculty scholarship shows that partnerships are at least somewhat woven into the basic fabric of the institution.

The majority of campuses responded affirmatively to all three questions, but their answers were not tied to specific partnerships and hence provide no information regarding the relationship between these three topics and the success of a partnership project.

Analysis of Community-Campus Partnerships

Campuses listed a diverse array of partnerships on their Carnegie application, with differences apparent both across and within institutions. A university's partnerships appear to be affected by a number of factors:

- *Campus size.* For example, more resources are available at a large university.
- *Mission.* For example, religiously affiliated schools are likely to be involved with faith-based organizations, and those with strong international ties are likely to have international partners.
- *Nature of the university.* For example, research universities are more likely to be doing research in or with the community, while comprehensive universities may be more heavily involved in working with K-12 students and teachers.
- *Areas of expertise.* For example, those with medical or nursing colleges are involved in health-related issues.
- *Demographics of the neighborhood.* For example, those located in the inner city of a large urban area are more likely to focus on poverty issues than are rural campuses.
- *History of the institution.* For example, campuses that have had extension units may be more experienced with sustainable community partnerships.

Partnership Complexity. Some community-campus partnerships were quite simplistic and limited in scope. For example, at the University of

South Florida, one faculty member and two students have been working with a community partner to evaluate a Web-based system for handling information from clinical trials. At other institutions, partnerships included hundreds of students and faculty and multiple community partners in possibly multiple settings nationally and internationally. For example, a University of Massachusetts Boston partnership funded by the U.S. Department of Housing and Urban Development Community Outreach Partnership Center involves more than four hundred faculty, more than a hundred students, and a community agency that represents more than twenty member organizations and companies.

Partnership Focus. Ninety-eight percent of the campuses had partnerships that directly relate to K-12 students or teachers. For example, Northern Kentucky University partnered with six rural school districts to provide their teachers in grades 4 through 8 with professional development related to inquiry-based teaching of science.

The other two most popular areas for partnerships were health (physical health, dental health, mental health, health education, and public health) and adult education (literacy education, workforce development, leadership development, postsecondary education, and related areas). Other focal areas were community planning, environment, economic development, government, courts and corrections, nonprofits, early childhood, museums and public history, and the arts. It also was not unusual for partnerships to cut across several areas. For example, Boise State University has a partnership with the Idaho Department of Environmental Quality and multiple small businesses to assist the businesses with environmental and other government regulations. This project has both environmental and economic development impact.

Community Partners. Campuses partner with all sorts of organizations, ranging from A (arts organizations) to Z (zoos), with literally hundreds in between. Although most partners are existing entities, such as school districts, businesses, nonprofit groups, and government agencies, some partners are informal assemblages, such as the local residents in specific neighborhoods.

The number of community partners ranged from one to more than a hundred. In some the partners are other universities; for example, Pace University is working on an environmental project with forty-four other campuses. A limitation of the data that was apparent when analyzing information about community partners was the ways in which campuses identified their partners. Some partners were identified only by their acronyms, making it almost impossible for those unfamiliar with the campus and community to understand the nature of the partnership.

Partnership Duration. The length of the partnerships ranged significantly. Slightly more than 20 percent of the campuses reported at least one partnership that was less than a year old, and two campuses reported partnerships that had been extant for more than a hundred years. The majority, however, were in the range of two to ten years. This may well reflect the time it takes to establish a working relationship that is the foundation of a functional, authentic partnership. In addition, over the past ten years, higher education leaders have increasingly emphasized partnering and community engagement.

Faculty and Student Involvement. The university partners are individual faculty or staff, groups of faculty and staff, academic departments or groups of departments, university centers and institutes, and combinations of these various groups. The number of faculty participating ranged from zero (which probably meant that the partnership involved only staff) to five hundred (probably the number who had participated over the forty years of this particular partnership). Most had fewer than ten faculty. For example, nineteen of the twenty partnerships listed by the University of Memphis involved fewer than ten faculty.

The number of students participating in partnership projects ranged from zero to several thousand, with the extremely large numbers reported for multiyear periods. Although campuses reported that both graduate and undergraduate students were involved in the partnerships, more undergraduates were listed. Graduate students were likely to be involved in partnerships at doctoral-granting institutions and particularly as community-based research.

Partnership Funding. Funding for partnerships came from a variety of sources: state and federal grants, foundation and corporate grants, contracts, partner contributions, internal university grants, and base funding. For more than half of the applications examined, the majority of reported partnerships had at least some external funding. However, it is likely that this reflects a bias in the partnerships selected for reporting. More typical partnerships involve faculty, community members, and students providing their time as "in kind" to achieve the goals of the partnership. In these cases, incidental costs are generally funded from existing budgets. (Resource questions are developed in Chapter Seven.)

Defining *Community*. The ways in which campuses define *community* can be inferred from their list of community partners. Partnering with a local community planning group suggests that the community is defined geographically (for example, the neighborhood around the campus); partnering with a group that serves Spanish-speaking immigrants indicates that community is being defined by social characteristics. Most campus community partnerships are relatively local, but some focus statewide and some are international in scope. The way in which campuses define community determines the types of partnerships it seeks. Campuses wanting to support and affect change in communities should begin with conversations that address how *community* will be defined.

Mutuality of Partnerships. Mutuality is a critical aspect of the definition and success of a partnership. Responses to Carnegie's question regarding mutuality clearly showed that campuses understand its importance within each individual partnership. Some universities promote its importance through training of faculty, staff, and community partners. Only a few universities described policies that relate to mutuality. For example, Wartburg College's policy on community engagement indicates a "commitment to *mutually beneficial* community partnerships" (emphasis added). The University of Kentucky's strategic plan states that "the engaged university also must listen to the communities it serves to fully understand their needs and ideas in the formation of responsive partnerships."

Applicants frequently reported ensuring mutuality through advisory or governing boards that plan and provide oversight for partnership projects. For example, the University of Pennsylvania's Center for Community Partnerships (CCP) has a twenty-two person community advisory board that meets twice yearly to discuss the Center's efforts, community concerns, and to solicit feedback on Penn's activities. Other applicants reported periodically bringing together representatives from the campus and the identified community to discuss issues relating to the partnership and its goals. These gatherings were sometimes informal and sometimes quite formal, with agendas and minutes. Whatever their form, such sessions serve as important opportunities for relationship and partnership building.

Campus Feedback to Partners. Effects to develop partnerships include other forms of campus feedback to partners. Only a few universities described policies relating to the feedback process, and even then, the policies were limited in their application. For example, Portland State University stated, "By definition, each Capstone must deliver a final product to the community partner. During these required community presentations students, faculty and community partners provide direct feedback and assessment of the project to each other."

Most universities suggested that feedback and assessment were project specific. They reported providing the community with one or more of the following: the final report from grant-funded projects; student evaluations for service-learning projects; annual reports; newsletters, magazines, and brochures; press releases; and oral reports at formal or informal partnership or community-wide meetings. Relatively few reported that they do not provide feedback or assessment to the community. What appeared to be missing from the applications was a systematic way in which campuses would engage in feedback. This challenge relates to other challenges of evaluation and outcomes, discussed in Chapter Five.

Scholarly Output from Partnerships. Articles, books, book chapters, and presentations were the most common scholarly products that were reported. This documents that faculty can be involved in partnership work and still satisfy traditional requirements of the academy. It also reflects, as discussed in Chapter Four, that reward policies continue to value traditional scholarly products and that the widespread acceptance of other products of engaged scholarship has not yet been realized.

NEW DIRECTIONS FOR HIGHER EDUCATION • DOI: 10.1002/he

Other forms of scholarly output were also reported, including curricular materials, theses and dissertations, radio and television presentations, technical reports, and grant applications. Some of the work was scholarship about engagement; some was the scholarly output from the partnership; and some of what was reported was output but not scholarly as defined by the academy (for example, making footage of a community event available to the local media).

Recommendations for Successful Partnerships

The Carnegie data show that the possibilities for campus-community partnerships are numerous and varied. Partnerships vary in their goals, size (number and type of partners, number of students and faculty involved), duration, focus, and need for funding. The key is for campuses and communities to work together to ensure that collaborations are beneficial to both. The following practical and experience-based recommendations are supported by the proliferation of successful partnerships discussed in the Carnegie applications.

Recommendations for Colleges and Universities. Communities, no matter how defined, offer rich opportunities to enhance student learning and faculty work. The opportunities can be overwhelming, however, because complex community needs generally exceed the capacity of any one campus. In determining which partnerships to establish or embrace, campuses should consider the significance of the problem that will be addressed and the resources and commitment needed to make a meaningful impact. Campuses may decide to focus on one area where they can make a significant impact by virtue of expertise or geographical location, while other campuses pursue a wider scope of partnership activity in accordance with a variety of factors, including size, location, and mission. Regardless of these decisions, which are made on individual and institutional levels and all levels in between, community partners agree that the key is for campuses to remain committed to the goals and expectations of the partnership. Community partners may look for signals of commitment such as the participation or buy-in of key campus decision makers or the willingness to have authentic give-and-take discussions beyond campus efforts where the inclusivity appears contrived or staged (Pasque, 2008).

Campuses with little experience in forming community partnerships may find greater success in building on existing and positive external relationships. Campus contexts vary greatly even among individual colleges, and the issue of context and culture becomes even more important when working with partners external to the academy. There are significant similarities between campuses and their community partners. Both are complex, heterogeneous entities comprising diverse groups with different priorities, goals, attitudes, and strengths. The demands on both exceed their resources. There are also critical differences between campus and community.

They have different cultures, speak somewhat different languages, have different calendars, and confront different demands outside the partnership. A mutual understanding and respect between potential partners is a firm requirement.

Recommendations for the Community. Colleges and universities are a source of knowledge and talent that can be leveraged in ways to benefit communities. As the Carnegie data showed, a community entity can partner with individual faculty, groups of faculty, departments, special centers or institutes, or even an entire institution. These multiple entry points can be an asset, but they can also challenge community partners that are trying to initiate a relationship or contact. The Carnegie data indicate that most engaged campuses have established leadership, whether more or less centralized, around community engagement opportunities. Community leaders can seek out these offices or start with existing contacts at the institution.

Partners must appreciate cultural differences among their organizations. For example, compared to the business or government sectors, campuses are less hierarchical, faculty operate with considerable autonomy, committees are often responsible for decision making, and the workday and work year are different from those in most other jobs or professions. The Carnegie applications clearly show that community and campus partners are able to overcome what may seem at the outset to be insurmountable differences.

Because universities are organizations concerned with the generation and dissemination of knowledge, campus partners are often interested in how a partnership can advance scholarship and student learning. When community partners are open to accommodating such interest and participation and work alongside campus partners to establish action or engaged research agendas, both partners have the opportunity to realize mutual benefits from the relationship.

Conclusion

Carnegie's Community Engagement Classification serves two equally important purposes: it evaluates university's engagement work and encourages more engagement. While care must be taken to interpret some of the reported data (for example, does "number of students" refer to the number in a single year or in the life of the project?), the applications provide a picture of incredibly diverse partnerships positioned to help address complex problems that require work from a number of levels and perspectives.

More can still be done to improve understanding of the quality of community-campus partnerships, in addition to what can now be stated on quantity. In selecting the partnerships that were put forward in their applications, campuses likely asked themselves a number of questions:

- How many existing partnerships were not described?
- On what basis are the listed partnerships representative?

- How do the described partnerships compare with those not described?
- Which partnerships were the most successful?
- What factors account for a partnership's being more or less successful?
- How was the partnership evaluated?
- What lessons were learned from the partnership?

Thus far, this critical discussion and knowledge regarding partnership quality have remained squarely at the campus level. A future study of how Carnegie-designated institutions decide which partnerships to report would add tremendous depth to this discussion.

Interest in community engagement has been growing exponentially in the past decade, and the Carnegie elective Community Engagement Classification both reflects the growing interest and fosters further growth. Mutually beneficial partnerships are a critical piece of community engagement because they offer advantages for both campus and community. Together campus and community can redefine their respective roles, together they can acquire funds that would be unavailable to either one acting alone, and together they can accomplish what neither one could do alone. The Carnegie data make it abundantly clear that no single formula exists for a community-campus partnership. Partnerships come in all sizes, focus on all sorts of subjects, and involve all kinds of partners. Their commonality lies in their relationships, characterized by mutuality, involving two or more individuals, groups, or organizations that share a commitment, and probably a passion, to achieve an agreed-on goal. Every campus and every community can find ways to make partnerships work for them.

References

Carnegie Foundation for the Advancement of Teaching, "Community Engagement Elective Classification." 2008. Retrieved December 15, 2008, from http://www.carnegie foundation.org/classifications/index.asp?key=1213.

Pasque, P. "Conceptualizations of Engagement: A Critical and Committed View of Collaborative Approaches to Community Change." Paper presented at the annual meeting of the Association for the Study of Higher Education, Jacksonville, Fla., 2008.

Tyler, J. B., and Haberman, M. "Education-Community Partnerships: Who Uses Whom for What Purposes?" *Metropolitan Universities*, 2002, *13*(4), 88–100.

CAROLE BEERE retired as the dean of graduate studies and associate provost for outreach at Northern Kentucky University. She continues to work on special engagement-related projects.

The Carnegie data offer important information about how institutions allocate funding for engagement and develop marketing and fundraising campaigns to support engagement activities.

Engagement and Institutional Advancement

David Weerts, Elizabeth Hudson

Research suggests that institutional commitment to community engagement can be understood by examining levels of student, faculty, and community involvement in engagement; organizational structure, rewards, and campus publications supporting engagement; and compatibility of an institution's mission with this work (Holland, 1997). Underlying all of these factors is campus financial commitment to engagement and whether engagement is reflected as a budget priority and key component in resource development campaigns.

This chapter examines ways in which engaged institutions allocate internal resources to support engagement and how these campuses have reshaped their institutional advancement programs (marketing, branding, and fundraising activities) to leverage financial support for engagement. We begin with a brief literature review discussing the relationship between advancement and engagement, followed by a formal investigation of how engaged institutions have approached resource development to support engagement programs. All colleges and universities discussed as engaged institutions in this chapter are recipients of the Carnegie Foundation's elective classification in curricular engagement and outreach and partnerships (Carnegie Foundation for the Advancement of Teaching, 2008).

Advancement in an Era of Engagement

Fundraising for public engagement programs has gained momentum, especially in the area of service-learning. Campus Compact (2004), a national coalition of over a thousand college presidents committed to engagement,

New Directions for Higher Education, no. 147, Fall 2009 © Wiley Periodicals, Inc.
Published online in Wiley InterScience (www.interscience.wiley.com) • DOI: 10.1002/he.359

has documented over seventy endowed centers for community and public service centers. Its guide suggests that institutions that have been successful in raising endowed funds for service programs share several characteristics: they have politically and civically active student bodies; enjoy strong support from administrators (especially presidents), alumni, and the campus development office; and operate service programs that are compatible with the vision, mission, curriculum, and goals of the institution.

More recently, traditional advancement practices are being reconsidered in light of the emerging emphasis on community engagement in higher education (Weerts, 2007). This may be fueled in part by research suggesting that today's higher education donors are less likely to give to advance institutional goals and more likely to give if their support yields tangible community outcomes (Strickland, 2007). In short, today's donors are motivated by giving opportunities that will make an impact on society (Grace and Wendroff, 2001).

Consistent with the desires and expectations of today's philanthropists, engaged institutions such as Portland State University have been highly successful in raising private funds for programs that are mutually beneficial to the campus and community. Engagement guides its goal setting, budgetary decision making, and priorities for its current capital campaign (Langseth and McVeety, 2007). And at major research universities, leveraging private support for public engagement fits squarely with federal grants programs that increasingly fund research on their merits in serving broad societal needs (Bloomfield and Wittkoff Kuhl, 2007).

Increasingly engagement has become part of the identities of these institutions, and the engagement brand has been leveraged to increase public support for these campuses. In particular, engagement as an institutional brand has been advanced to cultivate legislative support for higher education (Blanton, 2007). In addition, studies have shown a link between institutional commitment to outreach and engagement and increases in levels of state appropriations for research universities (Weerts and Ronca, 2006). Simply put, across all campus missions, engagement provides a platform to cultivate diverse revenue streams from private and public sources.

Advancement Practices at Engaged Institutions

To better understand budgeting and advancement practices at engaged institutions, we analyzed applications from a representative sample of U.S. colleges and universities receiving the Carnegie Foundation's elective classifications in curricular engagement and outreach and partnerships (Carnegie, 2008). We selected institutions for investigation by authority and control (public or private), geographical region (urban or rural), and mission (research or teaching oriented). Table 7.1 lists the institutions in our sample. Because institutional advancement concepts were integrated throughout each application, we open-coded (Strauss and Corbin, 1990; Jones, Torres, and Arminio, 2006) the entire document to capture relevant data.

Table 7.1. Institutions Examined in the Sample

Land-Grant Universities (Suburban or Rural Areas)	Private Research Universities (Large Metropolitan Areas)	Comprehensive Public Universities	Private Liberal Arts Colleges	Associate's Colleges
North Carolina State University	Emory University	Morehead State University	Rhodes College	Bristol Community College
Michigan State University	University of Pennsylvania	California State University-Fresno	Bates College	Chandler/ Gilbert Community College
Virginia Tech University	Tufts University	Western Kentucky University	Wartburg College	Middlesex Community College (Massachusetts)

Note: Land grant institutions: 1862 designated institutions, strong agricultural tradition in rural and suburban areas (very high research activity). Private research universities: private research institutions near or in major metropolitan areas (very high research activity). Comprehensive public universities: master's colleges and universities (larger programs). Private liberal arts colleges: four-year, private, baccalaureate colleges, arts and sciences focus. Associate's colleges: Associate degrees, public urban-serving campus.

Our analysis is limited by the type and number of application questions asked and how applicants interpreted and chose to respond to those questions. We also acknowledge that institutions vary in their capacity to support engagement, depending on the availability and range of revenue sources (public and private). Our analysis should be read with this in mind. Responses to the following application questions yielded the most data informing our analysis:

• Are there internal budgetary allocations dedicated to supporting institutional engagement with community? Provide evidence.
• Is there external funding dedicated to supporting institutional engagement with community? Provide evidence.
• Is there fundraising directed to community engagement? Provide evidence.
• Is community engagement emphasized in marketing materials? Provide evidence.

Findings and Discussion

To arrive at reasonable findings and conclusions, we conducted a thematic analysis of institutional responses to each of the four questions. Our analysis suggests that institutions are "finding their own way" in financing community engagement based on their own structures, culture, mission, and histories.

At the same time, a great deal of overlap in engagement and budgeting/ advancement practices exists across institutional types. We begin our analysis by briefly outlining how institutions allocate internal resources for engagement and then shift our emphasis to articulate how engagement relates to marketing and fundraising practices on these campuses.

Internal Financial Commitment. All of the institutions analyzed in our study demonstrated some level of internal commitment to fund engagement, broadly defined. In many cases, centralized administrative offices were set up to provide a clearinghouse for funding opportunities and provide a mechanism to manage this process. The scope and type of commitment to funding engagement vary somewhat by institutional mission, size, and how the campus collectively "makes sense of" engagement within its unique culture and setting. However, among all institutions, student-community engagement programs (such as service-learning) were a primary starting point for campuses to discuss engagement as a funding priority. That is, support for engagement largely focused on developing curriculum and student learning around civic themes. Furthermore, internal funds were often tightly coupled with a range of external grants (such as those of the AmeriCorps Vista Program) supporting a variety of activities and programs related to student learning, civic engagement, and student research opportunities.

Engagement budgets typically include staff salaries and benefits, student programs, supplies, and professional development for faculty and staff. Among all the institutions we studied, liberal arts colleges and community colleges appear to have the most seamless path of integration for financially supporting this work due to their emphasis on teaching and civic leadership. Wartburg College, when including its service-learning and curricular programs, spent nearly $1 million on engagement. And more than 2 percent of the Bates College operating budget goes to its service-learning center and public programming. In its budget, Rhodes College provides support for several diverse engagement programs such as Up Till Dawn, a student-run fundraising effort for a community hospital, and Rhodes CARES, an undergraduate research and service program.

Community colleges in our sample, such as Middlesex Community College, allocated percentages of their budget to engagement. In 2005–2006, the Middlesex Division of Social Science and Human Services spent approximately $6.8 million, or 16.2 percent of its total budget, on engagement-related expenses, not including additional funds for professional development. Furthermore, a portion of its student activities budget is used to promote civic engagement through college clubs, events, and an array of cocurricular activities.

Overall, private liberal arts colleges and community colleges are particularly well poised to provide institutional support for engagement through the lens of service-learning or student engagement programs. Since many of these campuses have a strong civic or teaching aspect to their missions, engagement programs are deeply embedded within the core teaching and learning philosophies of these institutions.

Not surprisingly, the budgets and range of internal support for engagement at research universities were larger and more complex. For example, Michigan State University has a general fund that supports the Office of University Outreach and Engagement with an annual budget of $3.6 million. This office houses much of the institution's engagement efforts, including activities of the National Center for the Study of University Engagement and the Center for Civic Engagement and Service Learning. Because of the varied aims and decentralization of engagement activities at research university campuses, funding for engagement at these institutions is complex, and the lines between internal and external streams of support are blurred. For this reason, it is difficult to calculate precise budgets for engagement. In an effort to quantify expenditures on engagement, Michigan State leaders calculated a salary investment of nearly $20 million for faculty and academic staff who reported their work related to outreach and engagement (calculated as full-time equivalent hours).

Finally, our analysis suggests that many campuses also support engaged scholarship in the form of internal seed grants. This practice is especially prevalent at research institutions. However, regional institutions such as Cal State-Fresno also provide mini-grants to faculty who connect scholarly activity with service-learning and civic engagement. In addition, one liberal arts institution, Bates College, offered competitive grants for publicly engaged scholarship through the Harward Center for Community Partnerships. In some cases, these internal grants were aimed at leveraging additional external funds for research.

Fundraising Efforts. Historically, elite private colleges have led the way in securing large gifts for higher education, so it is not surprising that these institutions are also leading the way in securing funding for engagement. The highest-profile example of raising private support for engagement programs is Tufts University, which recently secured a $40 million gift for its College of Citizenship and Public Service, now named for the Tisch family who provided the gift. Tufts leaders explain, "This gift is the third largest in Tufts' history and will ensure that students graduate from Tufts prepared to be active citizens in their communities and leaders engaged in addressing core issues facing society." The Tufts example, as illustrated in our data, is representative of many campus fundraising efforts that are college specific. The Tisch endowment funds a particular college focused on citizenship, and this gift may or may not be integrated with larger engagement efforts across the university.

Private liberal arts colleges have also made gains in developing fundraising agendas for engagement. Typically these efforts focus on student aspects of engagement such as service-learning. For example, in 2006, Wartburg College successfully completed an ambitious campaign of nearly $100 million that, among other campus priorities, supported community service and service-learning programs on the campus. In rare cases, small liberal arts colleges have woven their message of engagement into educational themes of philanthropy and citizenship. Bates College is particularly innovative in this domain. The college was one of the few institutions that have highlighted community work with alumni and other partners as potential funding relationships. Specifically, the Harward Center, the college's service-learning and community research center, teams with members of institutional advancement to identify and pursue fundraising opportunities relevant to their engagement efforts, for example, a National Day of Service where students and alumni collaborate to participate in community work. Bates College staff write, "While this kind of work is not immediately linked, at the time, to fund-raising for community engagement, it is part of a strategy of communications and involvement that is intended to raise giving for community engagement." In our analysis, liberal arts colleges were more likely to incorporate leadership development training with fundraising efforts.

Like the private liberal arts colleges, community colleges were most likely to align their fundraising efforts in the domain of service-learning. In some cases, however, community colleges relied on students themselves to raise support for engagement. On these campuses, students are finding ways to support their own projects and often are recognized by institutions for the work they do to this end. The application from Chandler Gilbert Community College illustrated the limited capacity of community colleges to raise money for these efforts: "As a small community college we do not have a dedicated development office for fundraising of this type. However, the campus participates in various co-curricular and extracurricular fundraising activities as part of our service-learning and community service events." Like students in liberal arts colleges, community college students were active in fundraising drives that benefited community-based organizations.

Land grant institutions are also making strides in raising support for engagement. At Virginia Tech, the current campaign casebook seeks a fundraising goal of $5 million to support engagement. North Carolina State embarked in 2005 on the ACHIEVE! Campaign with its $1 billion target fundraising goal. Of that goal, $88 million is geared to support extension and engagement scholarship and programs. At North Carolina State and many other institutions, fundraising directed to community engagement is often programmatic in nature, involving a partnership of the private sector, governmental sector, and the university.

Fundraising efforts for engagement are also under way at public comprehensive institutions. At Western Kentucky University, for example, one primary goal is to secure funding to renovate Van Meter Auditorium, a venue for performing arts and cultural and social events that bring together campus and community. In addition, the university's Kelly Autism Program was established with a private gift, and a second gift for the program has secured the financial resources necessary for its continuing operation.

NEW DIRECTIONS FOR HIGHER EDUCATION • DOI: 10.1002/he

In sum, the fundraising efforts of the fifteen institutions around engagement are wide reaching and diverse. In only a few cases, however, do the community engagement efforts of institutions relate closely with the institution's development office. Rather, fundraising for engagement is largely program specific and occurs within the departments or colleges for which engagement is a priority. Alternatively, students are also involved as fundraisers for engagement, but largely to the benefit of community organizations and their own leadership development. Rarely are student fundraising efforts connected to larger advancement efforts around engagement.

Marketing and Branding Engagement. Institutional fundraising efforts are clearly linked to campus marketing and branding activities. The institutions in our sample deliberately tout engagement as part of their institutional identity, as engagement is referenced heavily through external and internal media. Interestingly, we note that institutional marketing efforts were just as focused on bolstering internal support for engagement as external support. Internally, institutions discussed marketing for engagement as communications that focused on articulating civic engagement opportunities for current and potential students. For example, Emory University publishes a student brochure, "The Roadmap to Community Service," aimed at assisting undergraduate students who are interested in serving in the greater Atlanta community.

Overall, institutions employ a mix of marketing strategies to reach various internal and external audiences. Campus newsletters, alumni magazines, student handbooks, admission's viewbooks, and scholarship materials all sought to reinforce the theme of engagement at these institutions. The private institutions in our analysis typically had the most sophisticated and far-reaching communications materials articulating the civic activities of the campus. For example, the Rhodes alumni magazine carries frequent stories about Rhodes' civic engagement initiatives, and the University of Pennsylvania typically embeds engagement into its alumni communications. Penn writes in in its Carnegie application, "Penn's engagement activities are underscored in its alumni publications and have been emphasized at numerous alumni events." Furthermore, both Bates College and Wartburg College have an awards program to recognize alumni who exhibit outstanding service to their communities.

Differences in marketing engagement across institutions depend on the marketing capacity and the size and scope of the targeted audience. For example, in some cases, the institution's radio station is identified as a marketing agent, while other campuses must rely more heavily on local newspapers to publish news about the institution's work in the community. Some institutional applicants in our sample suggested that much of the external marketing for engagement focuses on building relationships with key stakeholders who benefit from and collaborate on engagement activities. Especially at major research universities, institutional leaders are frequently invited by government officials to make presentations on the institution's involvement in statewide, national, or international ventures.

NEW DIRECTIONS FOR HIGHER EDUCATION • DOI: 10.1002/he

As researchers, we observe that many of the larger institutions, both private and public, appear to be vying for space in the national and international spotlight of top engaged institutions. Private universities such as Penn and Tufts are likely to first position their work in a national and international context and then relate this to a local setting as well. Land grant institutions also view themselves in a national and international arena, but they are mindful about their primary responsibility to focus on the needs of their states. Alternatively, comprehensive institutions and community colleges may focus closely on regional constituents to show their presence in serving a geographical area. Finally, liberal arts institutions may seek to position their engagement brand to bolster their reputations as leaders in providing liberal education. Overall, we conclude that the ways in which institutions market engagement have a great deal to do with how they see themselves and define their key constituencies.

Campus presidents may be the most important marketing tools to shape the civic identities of these campuses. In Chapter Two in this volume, Sandmann and Plater articulate this point in depth, and we briefly reinforce the notion that presidential communication (on and off campus) is critical to reinforce the engagement brand. For example, we noted instances of campus presidents testifying before state legislatures on engagement (Morehead State University), at faculty assembly meetings (CSU-Fresno), and at Founder's Days (Virginia Tech). But the most powerful marketing strategy is evident through presidential behavior. For example, at Chandler/Gilbert Community College, President Maria Hesse actively participates in a broad range of business and community advisory councils and is a highly visible spokesperson for the role of the college as an active community partner. At Middlesex Community College, President Carole Cowan sits on over twenty community boards.

Conclusion

We conclude with several observations that inform our understanding of budgetary support for engagement and advancement efforts to support this work. First, student aspects of engagement are consistently present and promoted in fundraising efforts across all of the institutions we studied. Even at the major research universities where scholarship is paramount, student learning and civic engagement holds a prominent place on the institution's engagement agenda. In all cases, internal funding is largely supplemented by an array of grants from diverse public and private sources. Together these funds constitute the primary engagement budgets on these campuses.

Second, institutions have developed elaborate marketing strategies to communicate their unique brand of engagement. These brands are compatible with the culture and mission of each institution and help campuses communicate their values to diverse groups of internal and external constituents. At the same time, engagement is shaping and reshaping the culture of these campuses. Put simply, institutional boundaries are expanding to accommodate this emerging campus priority, and engagement is becoming part of the fabric of these organizations. Interestingly, we note the importance of the language used to describe engagement activities on campuses. Institutions are using many different words to talk about engagement, broadly defined. Our finding supports other studies suggesting that various engagement dialects develop around disciplines or campus cultures (Diamond and Adam, 2004; Wergin, 2006). In the case of advancement, it appears that institutions settle on a set of engagement terms that are most compatible with their mission and culture. In the end, campus presidents are primary marketers of engagement in both rhetoric and practice, and they can have a strong influence on the language that is used in this context.

Third, in the area of fundraising, campuses of all types are beginning to ramp up efforts to secure private gifts for engagement. Elite private institutions have a head start on raising money for engagement, mostly likely since they already have a sophisticated machinery to identify, cultivate, and solicit potential donors. Overall, however, fundraising for engagement is in its infancy and has yet to be fully integrated into campus priorities for funding. This is especially true at community colleges, where advancement is a relatively new enterprise, especially in the area of engagement. To date, engagement has not made its way fully into development offices as an institutional strategy to raise support.

What are the implications of our analysis for research and practice? Clearly, the topic of community engagement and its relationship to institutional advancement is ripe for additional research. As institutional budgets tighten, engagement offices will rely more heavily on alternative revenue streams to sustain their programs. Strong advancement programs are critical to providing resources for engagement, and new models must be developed and tested to provide mutually beneficial outcomes for both campuses and the communities they serve. Many questions remain about the implications of the growing engagement movement and its partnership with development offices. This chapter merely identifies themes from what administrators chose to include in their application; additional research on this topic can provide promising contributions to the fields of engagement and advancement.

Finally, our analysis suggests some important implications for institutional leaders. In particular, the potential benefits of collaboration between leaders of engagement and advancement are enormous; however, these connections remain largely unexplored. Engagement provides an excellent opportunity for institutions to reconsider the ways in which they relate to important external stakeholders: alumni, donors, legislators, and the public at large. We suggest that if marketing and fundraising are coupled with authentic institutional efforts to engage with community, the opportunities for raising support for institutions are tremendous. Institutional mission should be a compass that guides discussions about engagement and institutional advancement strategies.

References

Blanton, J. "Engagement as a Brand Position in the Higher Education Marketplace." *International Journal of Educational Advancement*, 2007, 7, 143–154.

Bloomfield, V. A., and Wittcoff Kuhl, M. "Institutional Advancement and Public Engagement in the STEM and Health Science Disciplines." *International Journal of Educational Advancement*, 2007, 7, 131–142.

Campus Compact. *The Service and Service-Learning Guide to Endowed Funding*. Providence, R.I.: Campus Compact, 2004.

Carnegie Foundation for the Advancement of Teaching, "Community Engagement Elective Classification." 2008. Retrieved February 20, 2008, from http://www.carnegiefoundation.org/classifications/index.asp?key=1213.

Diamond, R. M., and Adam, B. E. "Balancing Institutional, Disciplinary, and Faculty Priorities with Public and Social Needs: Defining Scholarship in the 21st Century." *Arts and Humanities in Higher Education*, 2004, 3(1), 29–40.

Grace, K. S., and Wendroff, A. L. *High Impact Philanthropy: How Donors, Boards, and Nonprofit Organizations Can Transform Communities*. Hoboken, N.J.: Wiley, 2001.

Holland, B. A. "Analyzing Institutional Commitment to Service: A Model of Key Organizational Factors." *Michigan Journal of Community Service Learning*, 1997, 4, 30–41.

Jones, S. R., Torres, V., and Arminio, J. *Negotiating the Complexities of Qualitative Research in Higher Education: Fundamental Elements and Issues*. New York: Routledge, 2006.

Langseth, M. N., and McVeety, C. S. "Engagement as a Core University Leadership Position and Advancement Strategy: Perspectives from an Engaged Institution." *International Journal of Educational Advancement*, 2007, 7, 117–130.

Strauss, A., and Corbin, J. *Basics of Qualitative Research: Grounded Theory Procedures and Techniques*. Thousand Oaks, Calif.: Sage, 1990.

Strickland, S. "Partners in Writing and Rewriting History: Philanthropy and Higher Education." *International Journal of Educational Advancement*, 2007, 7, 104–116.

Weerts, D. J. "Toward an Engagement Model of Institutional Advancement at Public Colleges and Universities." *International Journal of Educational Advancement*, 2007, 7, 79–103.

Weerts, D. J., and Ronca, J. M. "Examining Differences in State Support for Higher Education: A Comparative Study of State Appropriations for Research Universities." *Journal of Higher Education*, 2006, 77(6), 935–965.

Wergin, J. F. "Elements of Effective Community Engagement." In S. L. Percy, N. L. Zimpher, and M. J. Brukhardt (eds.), *Creating a New Kind of University: Institutionalizing Community-University Engagement*. San Francisco: Anker/Jossey-Bass, 2006.

DAVID WEERTS *is assistant professor in the Department of Educational Policy and Administration at the University of Minnesota.*

ELIZABETH HUDSON *is a doctoral student in the Center for the Study of Higher and Postsecondary Education at the University of Michigan and a graduate assistant at the National Forum on Higher Education for the Public Good.*

8

*This chapter offers suggestions for making an institution's compre-
hensive inventory of engagement activities more accessible and
useful for broader campus and public consideration.*

After the Engagement Classification: Using Organization Theory to Maximize Institutional Understandings

Courtney H. Thornton, James J. Zuiches

Campuses that pursue the Carnegie Community Engagement Classification
will in some form take full inventory of their engagement efforts in order to
address the range of questions posed by the Carnegie Foundation. At an
institution as large, diverse, and decentralized as North Carolina State University, this was no small undertaking. NC State's findings were carefully
consolidated into an almost ninety-page response to the Carnegie Foundation, and that summary included a great amount of detail on programs and
processes, yet elements of engagement were still missed (North Carolina
State University, 2006). This chapter further distills the findings into brief,
practical, and thought-provoking insights on the institution's approach to
university engagement using organizational theory to make the Carnegie
classification data more applicable and accessible to varied internal and
external audiences while also encouraging continued momentum and consideration of this work.

Bolman and Deal's four-frame organizational theory (2003) provides a log-
ical way to consolidate the data and documented findings from the Carnegie
process into structural, political, cultural, and human organizational factors that
interplay in the running of complex organizations. A campus that reframes its
Carnegie application data in this manner can further examine critical internal
consistencies across mission, priorities, budget actions, recognition, and internal and external communications (Holland, 1999). Reframing also illumi-
nates areas for improvement that require further attention. Finally, because

New Directions for Higher Education, no. 147, Fall 2009 © Wiley Periodicals, Inc.
Published online in Wiley InterScience (www.interscience.wiley.com) • DOI: 10.1002/he.360

75

individuals can easily relate to the structural, political, cultural, and human organizational aspects of institutional life, the act of reframing allows faculty, staff, students, and community partners to engage in ongoing conversations about institutional engagement in a meaningful and personal way.

In this chapter, we apply Bolman and Deal's theory (2003) to North Carolina State University's findings from the Carnegie community engagement application process. Each of the four perspectives serves to emphasize both areas of excellence in NC State's institutional commitment to engagement, as well as areas for improvement, while putting the data in a context that is useful for organizational consideration and decision making.

Organizing for Success: A Structural Perspective

A study of twenty-three colleges and universities and their commitment to engagement and public service found that organizational structure had the most significant impact on level of commitment (Holland, 1997). The structural perspective of organization focuses on the ways that coordination and control, specialization, and division of labor are employed toward the efficient accomplishment of organizational goals and objectives (Bolman and Deal, 2003). Two issues are at the heart of the structural perspective: how to allocate work (differentiation) and how to coordinate roles and units once responsibilities have been parceled out (integration). Universities are generally organized as professional bureaucracies with a small number of top administrators, a large number of workers who provide the organization's product or services, and few levels of management in between (Mintzberg, 1979). This type of flat, decentralized organizational model frees professionals to use their expertise but also complicates issues of institutional coordination and control. The Carnegie classification process at NC State revealed how existing infrastructure, division of labor, and policy can assist or constrain the university's engagement efforts.

The Office of Extension, Engagement and Economic Development is arguably the locus of engagement visioning and decision making on campus. This office is advised by a cross-campus administrative team. The structure for engagement radiates out to include the University Standing Committee on Extension and Engagement (USCOEE), a faculty-led committee; the Extension Operations Council of administrators; the Academy of Outstanding Faculty Engaged in Extension; and twenty-seven other operational units. These bodies are largely composed of administrators, faculty, and other professionals. While two students are selected as annual representatives on the standing committee and certainly have leadership roles within the Center for Student Leadership, Ethics and Public Service and the former Center for Excellence in Curricular Engagement, the widespread inclusion of students is not well supported by the current infrastructure. Indeed, Holland (1999) found that the greatest variation in institutional commitment to engagement was in regard to students; they were often an afterthought in the coordination process, with few institutions having explicitly defined expectations and roles for students in terms of engagement.

New Directions for Higher Education • DOI: 10.1002/he

Outside these leadership groups, NC State's engagement efforts are also structured by functional groups based on knowledge or skills, on products, around customers or clients, around place or geography, or by process. NC State also hires faculty with specific portions of their job responsibilities, up to 100 percent, designated in university extension and engagement and also hires graduate students specifically for extension assistantships. This role specialization and clear division of labor enhance organizational performance and help organizations achieve their goals and objectives more efficiently (Bolman and Deal, 2003). The division of labor has clear benefits for the engagement enterprise, including prompt and targeted response to community needs; however, this approach is not without criticism. Some view NC State's land grant mission as one of several organizational goals, while others see it as an overarching organizational philosophy. The first perspective accepts division of labor as appropriate, while the second perspective implies that all organizational members should be involved in engagement. These two perspectives have an impact on the way programs, units, and departments approach their structures for engagement, which in turn has an impact on the overall organizational structure. These types of philosophies may explain some of the variance in leadership structures discussed in Chapter Two.

Rules, policies, and standards are also key considerations of the structural perspective of organizations, as organizations are thought to work best "when rationality prevails over personal preferences and extraneous pressures" (Bolman and Deal, 2003, p. 45). Several guiding plans and policies at NC State aim to create consistency in aspects of the engagement process. Many extension- and engagement-related policies have been updated to better assist faculty. For example, in accordance with the recommendations in Chapter Three, reappointment, promotion, and tenure policies at NC State validate the inclusion of engaged scholarship and help individuals define and categorize their engagement work as they prepare dossiers and documentation. At large research universities like NC State, however, widespread commitment to engagement further depends on each college, department, and unit generating its own engagement-related terminology and policy for which it feels a degree of ownership (Lynton, 1995). NC State's tenure policy addresses the need for department heads, deans, and senior faculty to engage in such substantive discussions in reaching tenure decisions, but department- and college-level policies and practices merit further examination. Additional conversation is also needed to fully embed new meanings of "publication" and "peer" in the review process, as described in Chapter Three in this volume.

Managing Power and Resources: A Political Perspective

Organizations are lively arenas where coalitions of like-minded members come to bargain and negotiate for scarce resources (Bolman and Deal, 2003). The political perspective of organizations focuses on the importance of these

NEW DIRECTIONS FOR HIGHER EDUCATION • DOI: 10.1002/he

resources and brings to light issues of power and conflict. In order to advance an agenda such as university engagement, organizational members must understand who controls information, expertise, and rewards. They must also excel at "mapping the political terrain," building networks and coalitions, and bargaining and negotiating (Bolman and Deal, 2003, p. 207). In addition to resources, agenda setting and information sharing were key considerations of the political perspective related to NC State's engagement efforts.

As described in Chapter Seven, NC State has devoted internal resources to engaged programs, successfully supplemented those with external funds, and included engagement in campus marketing strategies. About 11 percent of the university's total budget is devoted to extension and engagement programming and originates from state appropriations, government grants, contracts and cooperative agreements, public and private foundation contributions, and fee-for-service arrangements. Engaged entities on campus have been successful at garnering additional external resources for their programming through sponsored extension projects. Resources for engagement are continuously sought at a number of institutional levels, such as major university campaigns and targeted college-based and programmatic fundraising efforts. As the funding of public research universities shifts increasingly to corporate partners and private individuals, NC State can expect impacts on the engagement enterprise similar to those experienced in the research enterprise (Rhodes, 1999; Slaughter and Leslie, 1997; Jaeger and Thornton, 2005).

External partners, whether funders or community collaborators, retain some control of the university engagement agenda. Organizations that include external perspectives in their decision making are more likely to change and take on characteristics of those external institutions (Greenwood and Hinings, 1996). Hence, significant relationships with community partners do and will affect NC State's engagement enterprise in a number of ways that should be acknowledged and considered. The engagement agenda is also controlled from within. The creation of the vice chancellor for extension and engagement position, as well as several coordinating committees and teams, has strengthened engagement networks throughout the NC State community. With more engagement-minded individuals networked together, the engagement enterprise should benefit from increased "access to decision arenas" (Bolman and Deal, 2003, p. 195). Existing engagement networks and alliances on campus and beyond can strategically consider how to expand their influence and share information.

Information is a key source of power in an organization (Bolman and Deal, 2003), which is why assessment and evaluation receive so much attention in the Carnegie framework. At NC State, departments, units, programs, and individual faculty members track and assess their engagement efforts in a variety of ways, from informal to sophisticated. This same diversity in assessment and evaluation approaches exists in regard to student outcomes

NEW DIRECTIONS FOR HIGHER EDUCATION • DOI: 10.1002/he

through curricular engagement. The wide range of approaches to assessing both institutional outreach and curricular engagement, coupled with NC State's size and complexity, makes it difficult to collect and use information that is both consistent and influential at an institution-wide level. Indeed, each of the instrument types described in Chapter Five in this volume are in use across the campus. Attention to this area will only grow, as those entities that can share information on engagement outcomes are more likely to gain additional power and resources for future engagement work. Assessment will also see increased attention as engagement components are formalized within accreditation processes, such as those of the Southern Association of Colleges and Schools.

Empowering People to Serve: A Human Resource Perspective

The faculty, staff, and students at NC State University bring indispensable ideas, energies, and talents to the engagement enterprise. The human resource perspective of organization focuses on how best to value these contributions to engagement through attention to various aspects of career and personal development (Bolman and Deal, 2003). The fit between the university's engagement goals and the individuals employed or admitted to the institution is of utmost importance in this perspective. As such, the goal is for engagement work to be meaningful and satisfying for individuals. Finally, this perspective purports that organizational members are motivated and inspired in their work when conditions allow autonomy and participation. The Carnegie classification process highlighted ways that NC State attends to the human resource perspective in achieving engagement goals, particularly through hiring, professional development, and collegial practices, as well as some areas for consideration.

NC State currently has 550 field faculty serving across North Carolina's one hundred counties and the Cherokee Qualla Boundary, a tract of tribal lands for the Eastern Band of Cherokee Indians. In addition, over 10 percent of on-campus faculty appointments specify a certain portion of time to be spent on extension and engagement activities. With significant numbers of personnel committed to extension and engagement, NC State's existing hiring policies and practices are key to ensuring that NC State finds faculty and staff who are committed to and motivated by its engagement mission. Institution-level acknowledgment of the importance of keen recruitment and hiring practices is foundational, but individual departments and programs must build on these to have a greater impact. When finding individuals who are a good fit for the engagement mission, NC State must identify and understand these individuals' needs and take steps to meet them. Engaged faculty need publication and presentation opportunities, funding, time for engagement pursuits, reward policies, and recognition. NC State attempts to meet some of these needs through specialized extension and engagement appointments. While this approach can empower those with extension appointments, it can also deter some without extension appointments from participation in community engagement. For that reason, the university's recognition of engaged scholarship through the academic tenure policy, seed grants, and support for other professional development activities is all the more important.

In contrast, the connection between engagement and student recruitment, admission, and enrollment is poorly understood and was not an explicit focus of the Carnegie classification framework. NC State can take additional steps to better understand the characteristics, behaviors, and perspectives of students, a significant pool of human resources that contribute to the university's engagement efforts. College students also have unique needs in terms of engagement participation and personal development. Curricular opportunities such as the Honors Extension and Engagement course encourage participation by meeting student needs for course credit and recognition. The former Center for Excellence in Curricular Engagement and Center for Student Leadership, Ethics and Public Service offer leadership development opportunities for engaged students.

While tenure, funds, and course credits meet some key needs of organizational members, these individuals feel further empowered and satisfied when they are informed, supported, and involved at all levels of the engagement enterprise (Bolman and Deal, 2003). NC State evidences a healthy respect for faculty autonomy and shared decision making, shown in part by the existence of several and varied learning centers, tutoring programs, extension services, noncredit courses, evaluation and training programs, library services, cultural offerings, and other programs and resources reported through the Carnegie classification process. The institution aims to inform new faculty about university engagement through the Connecting in North Carolina tour, a week-long trip through North Carolina that allows new faculty to see NC State at work across the state; however, not all new faculty are able to participate in this program each year.

Student engagement is thought to face similar barriers, with the perception being that only certain high-achieving pools of students are well informed about engagement opportunities. Indeed, the sharing of information is difficult at any institution as large and decentralized as NC State. From the initiation of brown bag faculty lunches to more targeted uses of technology with the student population, the institution can consider additional options for reaching a larger audience with engagement opportunities and ideas.

Living the Mission: A Symbolic Perspective

Organizational culture is "the way we do things around here" (Deal and Kennedy, 1982, p. 4). It is imbued in the collection of symbols, special language, stories, heroes, and rituals that help people find a purpose in and passion for their work and efforts. Research shows that institutional culture plays a significant role in a university's commitment to public service and engagement, as well as in the commitment of its organizational members (Holland, 1997; Antonio, Astin, and Cress, 2000). These studies find the highest levels of commitment to engagement among institutions that express a unique relationship with a community or region. They also find that as institutional prestige rises, this commitment level to community engagement drops. As a land grant university aspiring to the highest level of research achievement, NC State must balance these two competing forces in keeping a culture for engagement at the forefront. The Carnegie framework revealed that numerous and supportive cultural elements exist in NC State's core purpose and communication and recognition efforts.

The carefully chosen words of NC State's mission statement acknowledge its unique land grant status and historical commitment of university resources toward social problem solving. More recently, the university's 2006 strategic plan envisions the institution as an "engaged research university," placing two often competing missions side by side in relative importance. Several departments, units, and programs also include special language related to extension and engagement in their own mission and vision statements. NC State has recently and extensively documented its strengths and priorities for the future, several of which are related to community engagement, through UNC Tomorrow, a UNC system-level, holistic visioning process intended to result in North Carolina public universities' increased responsiveness to state needs. The system-level attention to engagement reinforces a supportive culture for this work and serves to advance the engagement efforts at NC State and other constituent institutions.

NC State also understands that it is not enough to perform the work of an engaged university; in the interest of organizational survival, it must also tell others about its efforts (Bolman and Deal, 2003). The Carnegie framework provided evidence of numerous marketing efforts aimed to inform both internal and external audiences that the institution is in fact living out its engagement mission. Through various publications and a robust Web presence, NC State uses both print and electronic media effectively in this regard.

NC State's culture for engagement is clear and recognized in other tangible ways, in the naming of campus buildings to the annual recognition ceremonies at all institutional levels. One example is the Academy of Outstanding Faculty Engaged in Extension, which honors university faculty and staff and actively enlists them as advocates, both within and outside the university community, for excellence in community engagement. Extension and engagement seed grants, facilitated by the University Standing Committee on Extension and Engagement, are given annually and motivate faculty and staff to develop ideas for innovative programs, enhanced external partnerships, and student engagement projects. These concrete actions are also symbolic: they serve to reiterate institutional values and beliefs and to perpetuate images of excellence and achievement.

Conclusion

While the Carnegie Community Engagement Classification afforded the NC State community the opportunity to assess its accomplishments and impacts, it also provided impetus to take a step back from the figures and programmatic details to examine the bigger picture: the underlying philosophies and processes that support engagement efforts every day but go largely unnoticed. This organizational analysis points to certain areas on a highly decentralized campus that merit more centralized attention, including student involvement, department-level practices, and assessment. These issues also cut across the four frames, so attention to these areas should have positive implications for strengthening the organization's structure, policies, human resource practices, and culture for engagement. Finally, the type of organizational analysis in this document serves to remind campuses of the nuances that are unlikely to be captured in an inventory or assessment but are nevertheless critical to the success of their engagement enterprises. Engagement efforts at colleges and universities across the country can be well served by purposefully attending to all aspects, both hidden and in plain view, of the structure, politics, culture, and human resources that enable institutions to fulfill this vital mission.

References

Antonio, A. L., Astin, A. S., and Cress, C. M. "Community Service in Higher Education: A Look at the Nation's Faculty." *Review of Higher Education*, 2000, 23(4), 373–398.

Bolman, L. G., and Deal, T. E. *Reframing Organizations: Artistry, Choice, and Leadership.* (3rd ed.) San Francisco: Jossey-Bass, 2003.

Deal, T. E., and Kennedy, A. A. *Corporate Cultures.* Reading, Mass.: Addison-Wesley, 1982.

Greenwood, R., and Hinings, C. R. "Understanding Radical Organizational Change: Bringing Together the Old and the New Institutionalism." *Academy of Management Review*, 1996, 21(4), 1022–1054.

Holland, B. "Analyzing Institutional Commitment to Service: A Model of Key Organizational Factors." *Michigan Journal of Community Service Learning*, 1997, 4, 30–41.

Holland, B. "Factors and Strategies That Influence Faculty Involvement in Public Service." *Journal of Public Service and Outreach*, 1999, 4(1), 37–44.

Jaeger, A. J., and Thornton, C. H. (2005). "Moving Towards the Market and Away from Public Service: Effects of Resource Dependence and Academic Capitalism." *Journal of Higher Education Outreach and Engagement*, 10(3), 53–67.

Lynton, E. A. *Making the Case for Professional Service.* Washington, D.C.: American Association for Higher Education, 1995.

Mintzberg, H. *The Structuring of Organizations.* Upper Saddle River, N.J.: Prentice Hall, 1979.

North Carolina State University. Final On-line Submission (MS Word). Carnegie Foundation for the Advancement of Teaching. 2008. Retrieved August 9, 2008, from http://www.ncsu.edu/extension/about/carnegie.php.

Rhodes, F.H.T. "The New University." In W. Z. Hirsch and L. E. Weber (eds.), *Challenges Facing Higher Education at the Millennium*. Phoenix: Oryx Press, 1999.

Slaughter, S., and Leslie, L. L. *Academic Capitalism: Politics, Policies, and the Entrepreneurial University*. Baltimore, Md.: Johns Hopkins University Press, 1997.

Thornton, C. H., and Jaeger, A. J. "Institutional Culture and Civic Responsibility: An Ethnographic Study." *Journal of College Student Development*, 2006, 47(1), 52–68.

COURTNEY H. THORNTON is director of research for the University of North Carolina system.

JAMES J. ZUICHES is vice chancellor for extension, engagement and economic development at North Carolina State University.

NEW DIRECTIONS FOR HIGHER EDUCATION • DOI: 10.1002/he

9

Community engagement is proving to be a force for diversification across higher education.

Will It Last? Evidence of Institutionalization at Carnegie Classified Community Engagement Institutions

Barbara A. Holland

When an innovative idea is introduced in higher education, Arthur Levine (1980) says that the new idea will inevitably meet one of four fates: enclaved, diffused, resocialized, or terminated. The determination is made by the individual and collective assessment of the faculty and leadership regarding the compatibility of the new idea with current organizational values and conditions. In no small part, that assessment is made based on self-interest: Do I want to take up this idea myself? Is it good for me or good for the institution? The successful diffusion of an idea or practice across an academic organization, that is, institutionalization, means it has moved from the margins of the institution to its core. In other words, the innovative idea is no longer considered peripheral.

Perhaps it is the long history of grant making and grant management in higher education that has made institutionalization the pinnacle indicator of success for new programs or practices. The Fund for Improvement of Postsecondary Education, for one example, was instrumental in creating a cultural value across academia regarding the importance of testing innovative ideas and measuring their impact by looking at the level of institutionalization. The emphasis on institutionalization as the best indicator of institutional acceptance of a new concept may be less scary than to admit that institutionalization is really just a long word that sounds much more academic than saying: "We changed!"

NEW DIRECTIONS FOR HIGHER EDUCATION, no. 147, Fall 2009 © Wiley Periodicals, Inc.
Published online in Wiley InterScience (www.interscience.wiley.com) • DOI: 10.1002/he.361

Community engagement has endured a long period of critical examination as an innovative practice in higher education, with some still questioning whether it is merely a faddish idea that will disappear with the retirement of the generation of activist-minded baby boomer faculty. Despite significant measurable indicators of growth in institutional commitment to community engagement (such as the growth of membership in Campus Compact, the number and diversity of institutions applying for grants from Learn and Serve America, and the introduction of engagement into regional accreditation processes), questions persist as to whether the practice survives only at the margin of academic organizations based on the temporary support of soft money, the strong advocacy of particular key academic voices, and current national attention.

The traditional question inferred by attention to institutionalization is, "Will it last?" or "Will it die out when we have a new leader or when the grant ends?" In the case of community engagement, attention to institutionalization reveals a more complex portrait of organizational change that includes a critical reflection on not only the institution's purposes but also the cultural values essential to the nature of engagement itself. The level of institutionalization is difficult to measure in part because the nature of community engagement itself challenges some of the traditional values and indicators of academic prestige and performance. This can be illustrated by a common faculty comment: "If it doesn't lead to a refereed publication in a top journal in my field, then I'm not interested." Such narrow and specific views deny the complexity and diversity of the ways academic organizations operate.

As a collaborative enterprise based on mutually beneficial knowledge exchange relationships between higher education and external communities, community engagement is not easily characterized by the traditional measures such as counting research publications in the disciplines, counting patents, or monitoring an institution's position in a comparative ranking scheme based on selective student admissions and research funding levels. Finding accurate ways to measure the impacts and outcomes of dynamic relationships that have intellectual benefits to the academy and practical benefits to community quickly becomes complex and more than a little confusing. If the essence of the work is collaborative, then attribution, costs, and benefits become much more difficult to define and measure. Yet measurement is essential. Every college or university must demonstrate the impact of its academic work, whatever the approach taken to accomplish the work.

The launch of the Carnegie elective Community Engagement Classification presents an opportunity to consider the impact of community engagement on academia, but perhaps not just through a focus on traditional indicators of institutionalization. The data reported by institutional applicants provide an interesting portrait of organizational change in action: changes that illustrate how community engagement is helping colleges and universities become more explicit about their missions, the learning environment that students experience, the design and rewards for faculty work, and the ways they develop and sustain dynamic partnership relationships with other entities. The process of measuring and reflecting on the implementation of community engagement may well be illuminating wider, more fundamental changes in tertiary institutions as they seek to improve and demonstrate performance and value.

Other chapters in this volume describe the details of the elective classification template and consider how institutions have responded to questions regarding the role of leadership and issues such as rewards policies, curricular activities, partnership models, and other aspects of institutional actions and strategies regarding community engagement. This chapter looks across all of these factors to consider how engagement is affecting the applicant organizations and what approaches seem to be associated with levels of institutionalization or, perhaps more accurate, organizational change.

In practice, the importance of specific factors and strategies to the institutionalization of engagement is largely determined by institutional type. While the Carnegie process is confidential and no applicants are identified in this analysis, a number of applicants have made their applications public. Readers seeking lessons learned on institutionalization would do well to look at the public list of those receiving this elective classification and identify institutions most like their own in terms of context, mission, and history, and then contact that institution to learn if its application is available.

Models for Measuring Institutionalization of Engagement

The need to measure the impact of engagement on college and university organizations has received considerable attention from researchers. A look at the literature on institutionalization suggests this attention was inspired in great part by a desire to establish how engagement can be institutionalized in ways that align with the need to create institutional capacity to adopt established principles and practices associated with quality engagement. In other words, community engagement requires change to organizational structures and values in order to ensure success. For example, if engagement relies on partnerships meant to promote mutual benefit and reciprocity, then external voices will be influencing the design of collaborative activities. This two-way model of designing teaching and research projects is new to college and university faculty.

One of the first frameworks for measuring levels of commitment to community engagement was the Holland matrix (1997). Holland is explicit that the matrix is a diagnostic tool "to describe and interpret the dimensions, approaches, and levels of institutional commitment to community service and service-learning and, thereby to facilitate institutional planning, decision-making and evaluation" (p. 33). The matrix directs attention to seven organizational factors that together characterize institutional choices and actions: mission; promotion, tenure, hiring; organization structure; student involvement; faculty involvement; community involvement; and campus publications. For each factor, the matrix offers indicators of four levels of potential commitment to engagement, from low relevance to full integration of engagement in the core actions of the institution (institutionalization). More recent and more detailed models include Furco's rubric (1998) for measuring institutionalization of service-learning as a specific engagement strategy and an institution-wide self-assessment tool developed by Community-Campus Partnerships for Health (Gelmon, Seifer, Kauper-Brown, and Mikkelson, 2005).

All of these approaches to measuring the level of an institution's engagement activities aim to accomplish at least three things: estimate the optimum or desired level of engagement activity that aligns with institutional purposes and capacities; direct attention to aspects of the academic organization that are essential to quality engagement; and identify specific areas of weakness where organizational change and capacity improvements are needed to support quality engagement. In other words, these tools are meant to help academic institutions develop an intentional work plan for institutionalizing engagement based on a critical examination of engagement goals and organizational actions. This is because engagement is contextual; it is necessarily influenced by community context as well as institutional history and the alignment between the two. This intentional exploration of context and capacity makes engagement a force for institutional diversification.

The design of the Carnegie elective Community Engagement Classification was influenced by these earlier tools, and now it has advanced the field by providing a template for the estimation and reporting of quantitative and qualitative data for each institution. This more detailed database will build over time to provide a much richer and more nuanced understanding of the impact of engagement on different institutions in diverse community settings and of the specific aspects of organizational change that may be most important and influential on institutionalization of engagement. Importantly, the Carnegie template is consistent with the foundation's commitment to classifying individual institutions in ways that avoid rankings or comparisons. Each applicant is asked to indicate its level of activity within the context of its own institution's goals. However, the Carnegie approach does not require the institution to report projected goals for full implementation: the reader cannot assess whether the reported level of activity is at 10 percent or 8 percent of the level of activity to which the applicant aspires. Some indication of intent can be inferred from the qualitative data offered. Nonetheless, the core factors that influence institutionalization remain the same, and some pattern of practice and implementation may be discerned. The analysis offered here may illuminate some effective strategies for embedding engagement while also suggesting the converse perspective: inattention to some of the factors may create risks to the sustainability of community engagement, especially in times of budgetary constraints.

Institutional Impacts of Engagement

Comments on institutionalization are organized below according to the major component parts of the Carnegie elective Community Engagement Classification template regarding institutional commitment and categories of engagement. Applicant data for each of the categories are explored in detail in other chapters; this discussion focuses solely on the apparent link of each category to efforts to institutionalize and then sustain engagement activities at applicant institutions. Even within some individual applications, there is variation in the answers provided that would inform institutionalization. These differences are influenced by institutional history and type, of course, but also by size (larger institutions face a challenge in being both succinct and complete; smaller ones can be more specific and detailed) or by the level of centralization or decentralization in the institution's approach to infrastructure, implementation, and monitoring.

Leadership. All applicants were able to cite the words and activities of their president or chief academic officer, or both, in supporting engagement. Institutionalization can be achieved or destroyed overnight by changes in the occupants of key administrative roles. In large institutions, this influence would be exerted by administrators at department or center levels as well. One of the greatest risks to institutionalization of engagement is leadership buy-in, support in word and actions, and demonstration of personal involvement. Ironically, too much rhetoric from the top can backfire if engagement becomes seen as one person's agenda. The descriptions in the applications of the growth in other leadership positions for engagement and the creation of engagement infrastructure seem to reduce the apparent risk of negative impact during leadership transitions. Some applicants described a recent leader transition and how that had been managed to ensure support for engagement. Others made it clear they included support for engagement in their leader searches, which seems the most effective strategy of all. Disappointingly, few applicants discussed trustee or board member involvement, which can be a worry as these individuals control the selection of leaders and the messages given to new appointees. This is an important but much neglected aspect of institutionalization of any innovation in higher education. A smart strategy is to give institutional leaders a regular report on engagement activities and make sure their speechwriters have lots of stories about projects and partnerships.

Coordinating Infrastructure. To centralize or decentralize is the question each of the applicants wrestles with in an effort to create an affordable and sustainable infrastructure that aligns with the specific institution's culture for managing innovative endeavors. Many institutions have moved

NEW DIRECTIONS FOR HIGHER EDUCATION • DOI: 10.1002/he

toward creating a midsenior-level engagement person, such as an assistant vice president or provost or the director of a significant office or center for engagement activities. The placement of these people and their units was not always clear, but there were examples of affiliations of infrastructure with academic affairs, student affairs, residence life, development, and the president's office, sometimes jointly affiliated. Leadership of infrastructure tends to reflect the placement in the organizational structure: those affiliated with academic affairs are more likely to have faculty leadership and so on. The scope of what is included in infrastructure ranges widely.

In decentralized models, engagement activities and projects may be divided among a number of areas of work, most commonly schools and colleges. In centralized models, the engagement center or office can be comprehensive or, more often, has a very specific focus such as supporting service-learning or coordinating partnerships. In regard to institutionalization, the important aspects of infrastructure seem to be encompassed in the intentionality of design and the link (formal or informal) to core academic work of teaching and research. Design issues affecting institutionalization include placement in the structure, access to top-level executive support, scope of the unit's responsibilities, qualifications of the unit's leader, and involvement of faculty, student, or community advisors. Given the diversity of designs described, the real message regarding the role of infrastructure as a tool for institutionalization is intentionality in the context of the political traits of the specific institution.

In many ways, the importance of careful design decisions regarding infrastructure has more apparent influence on the institutional reach and sustainability engagement than do sources and amounts of funding. Clearly the choice of placement in the structure is most successful when it has a specific rationale that is widely understood. If engagement goals are primarily focused on research and learning, a centralized model with academic leadership is more common. If engagement is more about student development and community relations, it is more likely to be placed in student affairs or external affairs units.

Internal and External Funding and Fundraising. For institutionalization purposes, the cultural tendency is to assume that internal base funding is a stronger indicator than external funding, which is more short term and thereby a source of vulnerability. In absolutely practical terms, that would be true; however, in the case of engagement, a mix seems to produce the best outcomes regarding institutionalization. A mix represents commitment from internal leaders for a sustainable base, but a robust array of external funding sources also suggests respect and accomplishment for the program as seen through the eyes of funders.

Given the nature of community engagement partnerships, a strong portfolio of external support should enhance institutionalization of engagement, in part because doing so aligns with traditional expectations that generating external income is respected and represents a return on internal investments that should be continued. Data regarding internal funds allocated for community engagement are equally tricky to analyze in that some applicants were quite literal in their focus on funding for specific and dedicated engagement positions or projects, while others set out a sweeping variety of activities that include many ways of directly and indirectly serving the public.

Large research universities often have a vast array of centers and institutes common to their institutional type, many of them with massive federal grants to support services. A few of the large university submissions listed dozens of these special centers, although the link to engagement was not always clear; others seemed to have applied a filter to report on centers where partnerships and knowledge exchange were conspicuously central to the goals of the unit. Medium and smaller applicant institutions were much more explicit in describing the funding linked specifically to a community engagement agenda. In some ways, smaller institutions are advantaged in institutionalization of engagement in that the work can be more focused and visible, and thus easier to observe, assess, and measure in terms of costs and benefits. Each grant or program is an exciting new development, and it is feasible for individual faculty and staff to directly observe the benefit or cost of engagement to their students or units. This is much more difficult in very large and complex research universities where thousands of students and faculty may be involved in a vast array of engagement, public service, and outreach activities. Monitoring activities and outcomes in a large setting is much more challenging, and the quality, cost-to-benefit, leveraged funding connection is more difficult to capture above the level of a single center or department. Of course, large universities have the advantage of some greater degree of financial flexibility and overall resource and disciplinary capacity to encourage a strong engagement agenda.

Finally, the link between engagement and fundraising is growing dramatically. This is an important return on investment for all institutions, as their involvement in community issues attracts the attention of philanthropists interested in those issues but not otherwise keen to give to a college or university. It is interesting to note here the growth in the number of colleges and universities with an endowment for engagement activities or a named, endowed infrastructure unit for engagement. Those seeking to institutionalize engagement would be wise to develop alliances with development, public relations, and foundation leaders in their institution.

Approaches to and Uses of Assessment and Monitoring. Assessing and monitoring engagement for institutionalization purposes is all about developing an evidence base. Data are essential to making the case for engagement, not just in academic or scholarly terms, though that is important, but also in terms of return on investment, impact on students, and benefits and outcomes for the institution and the community. Many sources of resistance and concern obstruct institutionalization of engagement. Applicants mentioned the need to inform program improvement and document benefits to student learning, links to fundraising and grant making, and impacts on faculty scholarship as reasons for collecting evidence. Assessment strategies focused almost completely on student outcomes, with occasional attention to community outcomes. Monitoring strategies were designed more as ways to track partnerships, projects, and activities than to gather impact data. Almost half of the applications examined reported they were still sorting out how to assess or monitor engagement. The most common approach to assessment is to integrate questions into existing student surveys or create a new one. Evidence is essential in advancing institutionalization, but only if the evidence is considered reliable and valid. Much more work needs to be done in this area to establish good models for different evidentiary purposes. Ultimately, efforts to build the evidence base must pay attention to impacts on students, faculty, partners, and the institution itself.

Engagement Definition and Plans. If engagement is integrated into strategic plans at any level of the university, institutionalization is enhanced, provided the plan is being actively used. There was much more evidence of integrating engagement goals into strategic plans than examples of well-crafted institutional definitions for engagement. The clear definition Carnegie developed for this process will most surely become the accepted definition and is already in wide use in the United States and other countries. More interesting in this analysis was the small number of institutions that have developed specific strategic plans explicitly for guiding community engagement activities. Where there are infrastructure units with significant responsibilities across engagement activities, there was more likely to be a strategic plan. As a strategy for enhancing institutionalization, a discussion of definitions and strategic directions seems to be underemphasized by many applicants. It is difficult to institutionalize engagement beyond early adopters unless nonparticipating faculty and staff can see the agenda and intended directions, along with a plan for monitoring and reporting outcomes, costs, and benefits.

Professional Development. Community engagement involves specific teaching, research, and partnership management skills. Not every faculty member has those skills based on their preparation, their experiences, and the intellectual focus of their scholarship. Professional development is a powerful tool for institutionalizing engagement at three levels: widening the basic understanding of engagement, motivating more faculty to take up engaged teaching methods, and developing a cadre of scholars doing research on and for the engagement agenda. All applicants could describe at least a minimal plan for engagement, even if it was just to send a few faculty to a conference on engagement. The majority of applicants have created at least a few basic training sessions for faculty on service-learning and partnerships or created peer mentoring programs, or both; others take advantage of professional programs offered by nearby universities, Campus Compact, or other organizations. The information provided suggests that most people want access to expert practitioners or scholars to provide professional development activities. The influence of peers from a particular discipline or comparable institution can be more convincing than an internal person. Applicants see professional development as important to institutionalization, but responses overall seemed cautious, probably because of the costs associated with such activities.

Community Voice. Applicant responses to this question were often quite brief. Community voice can be an extraordinary indicator of an advanced engagement agenda in that it can suggest the development of trusted relationships, but this is the dimension of engagement where higher education has far to go to learn new listening skills (Sandy and Holland, 2006). In a few advanced cases among the applicants, there was evidence of a dynamic, rolling dialogue and capacity for listening to community voice in ways that lead to direct influence on the college's or university's choices. The most common response from applicants was to describe various types of advisory bodies with community participation. Among these, some were written in a way that described quite explicit ways that community input from advisory bodies influenced the work of the institution in developing its engagement agenda. However, observers should be cautious of assuming that other applicants give less regard to community input; they may simply not have provided such a level of detail. Nonetheless, the reliance on advisory committees as a way of inviting community voice is quite dependent on compatible personalities to ensure a dynamic exchange of real voices.

Some applicants described innovative and dynamic models for developing public dialogues and public consultations as a way of assessing community needs and interests for partnership with the institution. The frequency of these would be interesting to know; if these types of open events are held too often, they could end up being driven by the same voices. The Carnegie elective Community Engagement Classification intentionality of invitations, formats, agenda development, and feedback mechanisms will be important to study as a way of identifying strategies that effectively strengthen the role of community voice in institutionalization.

Reward and Recognition of Engagement. Community engagement, defined in the Carnegie model as linking engagement to scholarly activities, cannot be institutionalized if there is not an explicit pathway for reward or recognition. Recognition has been dealt with widely through local faculty award programs and participation in national awards and recognition programs, straightforward ways to signal institutional support for the importance of engagement to institutional goals and priorities. More complex are the formal and informal reward systems that frame promotion and tenure processes.

Because reporting on this topic was optional in the first wave of Carnegie applications, the responses were interesting in that most felt that they could articulate a clear way that engagement could be included, evaluated, and counted in a promotion and tenure application process. Several have made specific revisions to policy to accommodate engagement. The more common and apparently helpful approach was to make more modest revisions that clarified guidelines to faculty regarding where and how to include evidence of engagement activity, that is, where engagement fits in the presentation of a faculty member's portfolio. Institutionalization would be enhanced if more institutions made the instructions clear and offered faculty not involved in engagement some training in evaluation of engagement activities as part of professional development.

Curricular Engagement. While some applicants made it clear that some of the numbers were necessarily estimates of student and faculty participation, the information provided here is among the most compelling concerning evidence of institutionalization of engagement. One could argue that the percentage of students or faculty actively involved in engaged learning courses could be the simplest and most straightforward indicator of institutionalization. If these data reflect the achievement of the desired level of engagement activity for the applicant institution, then many other aspects of institutionalization (leadership, funding, infrastructure, professional development) must necessarily be in place to a degree necessary to support the level of service-learning taking place. In the assessment of individual applicant cases, the data in this category offered a practical reality of how much engagement activity is taking place on the ground in the community. In addition, some applicants offered compelling detail about the links of these courses to majors, general education, learning outcomes, alumni surveys, and student retention.

Institutionalization is enhanced by the demonstration of connections between engagement and important institutional objectives (Furco and Holland, 2004) such as improvements in student recruitment, retention, fundraising, alumni loyalty, or learning outcomes. Although it was not possible in every case to discern where community engagement infrastructure was placed in the organization, it would be interesting to measure the relationship, if any, between the development of service-learning in the curriculum and the placement of engagement infrastructure in academic or nonacademic portfolios.

Finally, the two things that are hardest to change in any academic organization are promotion and tenure policies and the curriculum. A strong embedding of engaged learning in the curriculum across the spectrum of disciplines is a powerful tool for institutionalization, in part because engaged students are effective advocates for more community involvement.

Student Voice. The role of student voice often occurs spontaneously as students advocate for more engaged learning opportunities in the curriculum based on their positive experiences in a class with a community-based or service-learning component. Students who have a positive or negative experience with community-based learning can be quite vocal in influencing institutional commitment to engagement, and some of this was evident in a few applications.

Student voice also refers to the importance of considering students' self-direction in shaping and adapting to their community-based learning experiences. Similar to responses regarding community voice, this section mostly offered rather brief responses. The most common model is to link students to cocurricular programs such as service trips that occur over breaks in the academic calendar, local service activities, international study, special residences or living-learning communities, philanthropic events, or student leadership development programs. A few responses noted that students were involved in advisory or partnership groups. To date, student voice influences institutionalization mostly through demands for more service-learning opportunities. Student voice, while associated with institutionalization and quality of engagement, seems most likely to occur in institutional contexts that already value student voice across the learning experience and university organization.

Scholarship from Curricular Engagement. Because the request was specifically for scholarship (research, publications, presentations) arising from faculty consideration of engaged teaching and learning practices, this section of the template has two interesting influences on institutionalization. Recognizing and exploring these works reinforces the notion of the connection of engagement to teaching and learning while also encouraging the scholarship of teaching and learning. These contribute to institutionalization by giving involved faculty research and publication credits while also improving their teaching. However, the template does not explicitly provide for reporting of engaged research. Although it is difficult to imagine a way to do so without triggering a massive submission of the rapidly growing arena of community-based research, recognition of the role of engagement in both teaching and research is important to faculty achievement and professional recognition and therefore would be valuable in advancing institutionalization. For example, some colleges and universities have observed that service-learning partnerships have led to some new opportunities for community-based research projects leading to grants and publications.

Outreach and Partnership. Including this section in the Carnegie template was helpful not just because some institutions use *outreach* or other terms to describe activities others might call *engagement*, but, more important, because there is a benefit to describing and honoring more traditional ways that colleges and universities interact with communities.

While community engagement is defined as a two-way activity characterized by mutually beneficial exchange of knowledge in a context of partnership and reciprocity (the Carnegie definition), other forms of providing free or fee-based services, events, facilities, and programs for public consumption are valid and important indicators of a comprehensive relationship between an institution and external stakeholders. By defining categories and subcategories of community-related activity, the Carnegie template is illustrating the range of activities that institutions may pursue while also reinforcing the mutually beneficial nature of community

NEW DIRECTIONS FOR HIGHER EDUCATION • DOI: 10.1002/he

engagement as a specific form of scholarship linked to core teaching, learning, and research activities.

Although many public service and outreach activities are not truly engagement (though many could be with the introduction of knowledge exchange partnerships), reporting on these illustrates the range of work and honors those faculty or staff who are concerned that traditional activities will not be valued or rewarded if engagement concepts are seen as more valued or important. Doing so can enhance institutionalization by reducing conflict and confusion over what is or is not engagement.

As the body of Carnegie data grows, it may be useful to query the data to explore potential links between relationship types and the connection of one-way public services to the development of academically engaged partnerships, or the reverse. Over time, the Carnegie approach should lead to greater clarity and regard for different models of connecting academic institutions to external constituencies; all are important and valuable, but only some are community engagement, and the difference must be understood to facilitate institutionalization.

Conclusion

Clearly, applicant institutions seek to institutionalize engagement primarily through a focus on aspects of organizational structure and culture traditionally associated with sustainability of any new initiative: infrastructure, curricular reform, funding, leadership, and policies. Common sense and past research (Birnbaum, 1988) tell us that advocates for change in an institution target the strategies perceived to be most influential with the most people, often revealed by what worked well in previous situations when change occurred successfully.

In any one case, the emphasis given to one or more of these factors over the others is most likely a reflection of institutional history. For example, although there are exceptions, community engagement was originally of most intense interest to colleges and universities not in the most prestigious ranks. Many of these institutions found the exploration of engagement to be useful in developing a more local, specific, and compelling vision and mission than that offered by imitation of already successful elite institutions (Holland, 2005). Thus, the exploration of engagement proved to generate corollary benefits to overall institutional culture and operations.

In other words, as engagement is implemented more widely across higher education, it seems to be acting as a force for enhancing institutional diversity. This should not be surprising given that the development of effective knowledge exchange relationships that involve community, students, and faculty in the co-generation and application of knowledge mandates greater intentionality and coherence in each partner organization. If partnerships are to succeed, each partner must know what it wants from and what it has to give to the partnership. Community engagement involves others outside academia in the work of teaching, learning, research, dissemination, and application. To do this well requires higher education to develop new skills and capacities of collaboration and cooperation. The analysis of the first wave of Carnegie elective classification applicants suggests that these changes will likely alter not only higher education's external relationships, but its core internal traditions as well—eventually. The degree to which engagement can weather changes in leadership or budgetary support will probably remain the ultimate indicator of institutionalization.

These signs that institutionalizing engagement is leading to cultural and organizational change align well with new conceptions of knowledge production and dissemination (Gibbons and others, 1994) that recognize that anyone with Internet access can self-declare to be a researcher and publish important new knowledge. The world's universities are important producers of new knowledge, but many other sources of new knowledge for many purposes lie beyond the enhancement of the disciplines. The role of the higher education sector is changing as the world becomes more diverse and interconnected. The forthcoming exit of the baby boomer faculty generation will open the door for a new generation of academics who will reflect this more global world. We already see signs that these new scholars want to engage in knowledge activities that address global and local issues, and they want to work in collaborative modes (Trower, 2006).

Carnegie's attention to the development of engagement across higher education reinforces the notion of institutional distinctiveness, and the process also reveals a great deal about how change occurs in academic organizations. Ultimately the idea of community engagement as a distinct strategy may disappear as it is blended into a new twenty-first-century conception of academic culture that links tertiary students and faculty with external partners in dynamic models of working with knowledge that blend the processes of teaching, learning, discovery, and application in ways even more integrative than Boyer (1990) predicted. Engagement may be perceived as a confronting challenge to some of the most traditional values of academia, but the distinctive stories told through this first wave of the Carnegie process suggest a thoughtful and organic process that may be leading toward the creation of a more diverse array of respected academic cultures with different values and scholarly environments that will align well with a complex world that has increasingly dynamic and urgent knowledge needs.

References

Birnbaum, R. *How Colleges Work: The Cybernetics of Academic Organization and Leadership*. San Francisco: Jossey-Bass, 1988.

Boyer, E. *Scholarship Reconsidered: Priorities of the Professoriate*. San Francisco: Carnegie Foundation for the Advancement of Teaching, 1990.

Furco, A. *Self-Assessment Rubric for the Institutionalization of Service-Learning in Higher Education*. Berkeley: Service-Learning Research and Development Center, University of California at Berkeley, 1998.

Furco, A., and Holland, B. A. "Institutionalizing Service-Learning in Higher Education: Issues and Strategies for Chief Academic Officers." In M. Langseth and W. Plater (eds.), *Public Work and the Academy: A Guidebook for Academic Administrators on Civic Engagement and Service-Learning.* San Francisco: Anker/Jossey-Bass, 2004.

Gelmon, S. B., Seifer, S. D., Kauper-Brown, J., and Mikkelsen, M. *Community-Engaged Scholarship for Health Collaborative: Institutional Self-Assessment.* Seattle: Community-Campus Partnerships for Health, 2005.

Gibbons, M., and others. *The New Production of Knowledge: The Dynamics of Science and Research in Contemporary Societies.* Thousand Oaks, Calif.: Sage, 1994.

Holland, B. A. "Analyzing Institutional Commitment to Service: A Model of Key Organizational Factors." *Michigan Journal of Community Service Learning,* 1997, 4, 30–41.

Holland, B. A. "Institutional Difference in Pursuing the Public Good." In A. J. Kezar and Associates (eds.), *Higher Education for the Common Good: Emerging Voices from a National Movement.* San Francisco: Jossey-Bass, 2005.

Levine, A. *Why Innovation Fails: The Institutionalization and Termination of Innovation in Higher Education.* Albany: State University of New York Press, 1980.

Sandy, M., and Holland, B. (2006). "Different Worlds and Common Ground: Community Partner Perspectives on Campus-Community Partnerships." *Michigan Journal of Community Service Learning.* 13, 30–43.

Trower, C. "Gen X Meets Theory X: What New Faculty Want." Presentation at the Thirty-Third National Conference of the National Center for the Study of Collective Bargaining in Higher Education and the Professions, New York, 2006.

BARBARA A. HOLLAND *directs the U.S. National Service Learning Clearinghouse and serves as pro vice-chancellor engagement, Office of University Engagement, Campbelltown Campus, University of Western Sydney, Australia.*

NEW DIRECTIONS FOR HIGHER EDUCATION • DOI: 10.1002/he

10

What are the experiences, outcomes, and lessons learned from the first wave of Carnegie classified community-engaged institutions?

The First Wave of Community-Engaged Institutions

Lorilee R. Sandmann, Courtney H. Thornton, Audrey J. Jaeger

In nature, waves are transmitters of energy. Once the energy moves through the medium, that medium often returns to its previous state. The first wave of community-engaged institutions has transmitted great energy across the U.S. higher education system. And in contrast to what occurs in nature, these classified institutions often do not go back to the way they were before the designation.

The Carnegie process frequently served as the tool that forced an institution to change direction. For example, the University of South Florida discovered through the classification application process that improvements were needed to strengthen its curricular engagement efforts. It has since moved forward on its own findings. The application process helped Otis College to solidify the language that has come to identify its unique mission and approach in the community. Furthermore, the classification process provided support for a major curricular transformation that involved community partners, transdisciplinarity, and new ways of thinking about the practice of engaged teaching in the fine arts.

Just like waves in the ocean, the Carnegie classified institutions reviewed in this volume are unique and are exhibiting constant motion, new shapes and forms, and the potential to transform their environments. Indeed, transition is one of the major themes evident throughout the chapters. Whether in leadership, promotion and tenure policies and practice, or fundraising, many of the campuses indicated that they had made progress but envisioned additional change.

NEW DIRECTIONS FOR HIGHER EDUCATION, no. 147, Fall 2009 © Wiley Periodicals, Inc.
Published online in Wiley InterScience (www.interscience.wiley.com) • DOI: 10.1002/he.362

To provide predictability and reliability, the Carnegie framework was only minimally revised in the 2008 classification round and will not be changed for the next round as well. Nevertheless, in anticipation of the continuing wave of change, we offer the following considerations in institutional practice and potential adjustments in the framework that may be considered for future classification efforts.

Emerging and Needed Best Practices in Community Engagement

The Community Engagement Classification framework essentially defines the areas where a campus can find evidence if it has institutionalized engagement. Indeed, campuses provided this evidence in abundance, and chapter authors synopsized and analyzed the huge inventory of ideas and practices included in the applications. As Sandmann and Plater highlight in Chapter Two, leadership matters, particularly executive leadership and including leadership by key faculty members. Also, successful institutions are those with some infrastructure (positional or structural) to support engagement activities. Weerts and Hudson note in Chapter Seven that purposeful advancement strategies are critical to providing the necessary resources for engagement activities to be sustained as well as develop. Funders will inevitably require institutions and campus partners to evaluate community-engaged practices. Furco and Miller suggest in Chapter Five that campuses move toward more comprehensive, longitudinal assessment plans. These plans include authentic forms of evidence such as student products that capture student learning in a community-engaged course, as Bringle and Hatcher also suggest in Chapter Four. Institutions on the forefront of engagement, according to Saltmarsh, Giles, Ward, and Buglione in Chapter Three, are constructing policies that reward community engagement across the faculty roles and including and valuing community partners in the peer review process. Best practices for community-campus partnerships, as Beere described in Chapter Six, include those that consider the ideas set out here and have a clear focus and direction that coincide with the culture and mission of the community partner and campus. Thornton and Zuiches, in Chapter Eight, suggest that those institutions who use their findings as a springboard for strategic planning will be best positioned to continue their progress.

These analyses are only the first step required on the path of recognizing and defining the meaningful and useful best practices that many desire to know. Engagement leaders must continue to identify any gaps in how we understand or identify the institutionalization of engagement, attend to differences in institutional types and missions, and move these initial analyses further toward issues of quality and standards.

Areas for Future Progress. The institutions, in their applications, confirmed several fundamental areas that continue to challenge how engagement is enacted, communicated, and understood across the country. One such area is recognizing and documenting the authentic involvement of community partners in outreach and engagement efforts. As both Driscoll, and Saltmarsh, Giles, Ward, and Buglione, noted in their chapters, institutions found it difficult to discuss reciprocity in their community relationships and understand how that central component of engaged scholarship might be documented for purposes of faculty rewards. The fact that institutions most frequently communicated university-outbound activities rather than community-to-university-inbound programs is another indicator that the idea of reciprocity may deserve additional attention in the nationwide conversation on engagement. In fact, there was a clear, consistent void in relation to community input and voice across the applications submitted to Carnegie. Driscoll challenged institutions to develop new understandings with communities; these new partnerships would demand new skills and a new way of conceptualizing community.

A second consideration, and one that is not new, is that of the vocabulary of engagement. The Carnegie classified institutions varied widely in their consideration of the terms *community engagement, curricular engagement*, and *outreach*. Although this volume does not include an examination of the nuances of engagement language, the applications could certainly provide such information. One potential outcome of the Carnegie classification could be a consolidation or typology of engagement language use that might come to assist institutions across the country in communicating engagement ideals, efforts, and achievements to stakeholders, both internal and external.

A third and critical area requiring attention and progress is that of assessment. Within the Carnegie applications, there is little evidence at the program or institutional level of outcomes and no longitudinal perspectives offered. What is fairly unknown about the engagement efforts described by classified institutions is who is benefiting the most and the least, whether these engaged efforts are the most efficient way to address community issues and concerns, and whether these efforts are leading to sustained community change. In a time of demands for accountability in higher education, the limited linkage of engagement with evaluation, outcomes, or accreditation of postsecondary education is striking. It remains to be seen how the Carnegie classified institutions in the first wave have been prompted through the application process to pay greater attention to this area. Indeed it is noted within the chapters that the assessment process itself is a critical part of the institutionalization of community engagement. As the framework quickly becomes an evaluation tool for many campuses, more work is needed to adjust both the framework and the campuses for this expectation. Any progress made in improving assessment would have great potential to create a ripple effect at institutions across the country, as well as to affect how the Carnegie framework addresses this area in the future.

The Evolution of the Framework

While progress on reciprocity, definitions, and assessment must move forward on individual campuses, other change may be required of the framework itself.

Driscoll notes in Chapter One that the framework for the elective classification in community engagement was designed to respect and honor the diversity of institutions of higher education, as well as their approaches to community engagement. We agree that the initial set of awardees is diverse in type and effort; however, the overarching classification may still need to progress further to fully recognize the diversity of approaches to engagement. For example, it may be important to note institutions that adopt a geographical focus in their engagement efforts, such as a local community or a region. This type of further distinction, a more mission-focused strategy, would both align with Carnegie's approach to other classifications as well as provide campuses with more meaningful and ready peers for comparison and analysis.

Furthermore, the current framework suggests that all recognized engaged institutions are of the same quality. Self-reported data for other Carnegie classification types are based on clear, objective measures, whereas the elective classification in engagement offers institutions the opportunity to distinguish between what they chose to report and what they chose not to include. This self-selection process allows diversity and uniquenesses to be highlighted to some extent, but it also lacks objectivity and consistent quality measures.

As a second set of community-engaged institutions is classified, the Carnegie Foundation for the Advancement of Teaching has chosen to eliminate the separate distinctions for curricular engagement and outreach and partnerships, noting that institutions that receive the community-engaged distinction should be addressing both of these areas. This idea connects to Holland's suggestion that community engagement as a distinct strategy may disappear as more institutions are classified and the academic culture moves toward a model that blends the processes of teaching, learning, discovery, and application. Thus, the need for the separate classification would no longer be necessary given the predominant acceptance of community engagement as the optimal means to achieve societal goals. If the classification is to remain useful on its own, then it must evolve in a way that balances recognition with opportunities for differentiation and quality oversight.

As colleges and universities continue to look for evidence of how they encourage, value, and sustain engagement, the framework and applications may be found to virtually ignore important areas that contribute to institutionalization and that are worthy of separate consideration. Graduate education and preparation is one such area that has already been identified (O'Meara, 2007).

Finally, the applications to the Carnegie Foundation were highly marketing oriented. The process offered institutions the opportunity to publicize accomplishments and share best practices. Through the rich evidence put forth in the Carnegie applications, we know that campuses seeking to institutionalize engagement would be astute to develop alliances with public relations specialists, foundation leaders, and development officers. In Chapter Nine, Holland notes that this is an area where much more work needs to be done so as to establish good models of sustaining the engagement movement. Yet these alliances must be balanced with strict attention to the ultimate societal purposes of community engagement.

This marketing orientation may actually signal the institutionalization of community engagement and that analytical methods of strategic management are emerging: best practices, business planning, competition, funding, and strategic planning and partnerships, for example. Yet this public relations focus also may be viewed as implying a lack of attention to sustained social change by institutions in their engagement efforts. The evidence presented in the applications must ultimately be found consistent with outcomes of strengthened civic awareness and responsibility of students, enhanced community, and campus capacity to work in partnership to address critical social issues, and, fundamentally, improved societal conditions and transformed higher education institutions. Again, this initial analysis can move the framework one step closer to including more clear and objective measures that alleviate some of this concern.

Riding the Wave of Momentum

Although it is important to consider the impacts of the Carnegie Community Engagement Classification on individual institutions, we must also consider the cumulative effect of this wave of classified institutions. Many of these changes remain to be seen, but some early indications are that the classification is contagious. For example, in the sixteen-campus public university system of North Carolina, two institutions were classified in 2006 and ten sister institutions applied in 2008, all but two achieving the classification. The Carnegie data show that the engagement movement is more than one campus partnering with community organizations to provide students with unique learning opportunities. Instead, engagement can be viewed as a statewide initiative to address societal issues as in North Carolina, Kentucky, and other states. Indeed a national picture of engagement is evolving as 119 additional colleges and universities were successfully classified as community-engaged institutions in 2008. Another 28 institutions applied for the distinction. Almost all states are represented by the engaged institutions, thus offering a national perspective on engagement.

The national perspective is one that we believe requires further refining. The Community Engagement Classification has helped us capture critical information at a time when a similar set of changes is occurring across multiple institutions. With that magnitude of change under way, citizens expect to see results to the world's biggest problems emanating from higher education institutions. However, this movement is still fluid and we must acknowledge that leadership transitions, economic crises, and shifts in national public policy may either threaten or support the forward progress of this wave. We can accelerate the amplified impacts of this change movement only by envisioning "next steps" that provide needed consistency, ensure open collaboration on important social issues, and harness the full potential of a network of engaged colleges and universities. The Community Engagement Classification should motivate collective institutions to come together to develop new model or models of collaborative leadership for real social progress. We cannot afford not to do so.

We hope that the energy created by this first collective wave of classified institutions, as well as those recently classified, will inspire continuous change and forward motion in the nationwide efforts to heighten the value and focus on higher education engagement.

Reference

O'Meara, K. (2007, February). "Graduate Education and Civic Engagement." NERCHE Working Brief #20, pp. 1–8. Retrieved July 1, 2009, from www.nerche.org/briefs/NERCHE_Brief_20_Graduate_Education_and_Civic_Engagement.doc

LORILEE R. SANDMANN is associate professor in the Department of Lifelong Education, Administration and Policy at the University of Georgia and director of the National Review Board for the Scholarship of Engagement.

COURTNEY H. THORNTON is director of research for the University of North Carolina system.

AUDREY J. JAEGER is associate professor of higher education and founder of the Center for Research on Engagement at North Carolina State University.

NEW DIRECTIONS FOR HIGHER EDUCATION • DOI: 10.1002/he

INDEX

NEW DIRECTIONS FOR HIGHER EDUCATION

ORDER FORM SUBSCRIPTION AND SINGLE ISSUES

DISCOUNTED BACK ISSUES:

Use this form to receive 20% off all back issues of *New Directions for Higher Education*.
All single issues priced at **$23.20** (normally $29.00)

TITLE	ISSUE NO.	ISBN

Call 888-378-2537 or see mailing instructions below. When calling, mention the promotional code JBXND to receive your discount. For a complete list of issues, please visit www.josseybass.com/go/ndhe

SUBSCRIPTIONS: (1 YEAR, 4 ISSUES)

☐ New Order ☐ Renewal

U.S.	☐ Individual: $89	☐ Institutional: $244
CANADA/MEXICO	☐ Individual: $89	☐ Institutional: $284
ALL OTHERS	☐ Individual: $113	☐ Institutional: $318

Call 888-378-2537 or see mailing and pricing instructions below.
Online subscriptions are available at www.interscience.wiley.com

ORDER TOTALS:

Issue / Subscription Amount: $ _____

Shipping Amount: $ _____
(for single issues only – subscription prices include shipping)

Total Amount: $ _____

SHIPPING CHARGES:

	SURFACE	DOMESTIC	CANADIAN
First Item		$5.00	$6.00
Each Add'l Item		$3.00	$1.50

(No sales tax for U.S. subscriptions. Canadian residents, add GST for subscription orders. Individual rate subscriptions must be paid by personal check or credit card. Individual rate subscriptions may not be resold as library copies.)

BILLING & SHIPPING INFORMATION:

☐ **PAYMENT ENCLOSED:** *(U.S. check or money order only. All payments must be in U.S. dollars.)*

☐ **CREDIT CARD:** ☐ VISA ☐ MC ☐ AMEX

Card number _____ Exp. Date _____

Card Holder Name _____ Card Issue # *(required)* _____

Signature _____ Day Phone _____

☐ **BILL ME:** *(U.S. institutional orders only. Purchase order required.)*

Purchase order # _____
Federal Tax ID 13559302 • GST 89102-8052

Name _____

Address _____

Phone _____ E-mail _____

Copy or detach page and send to: **John Wiley & Sons, PTSC, 5th Floor**
989 Market Street, San Francisco, CA 94103-1741

Order Form can also be faxed to: **888-481-2665**

PROMO JBXND